THE GRAND CANYON ZEN GOLF TOUR

A MEMOIR BY JACK RANDOM

Featuring
The Handbook of Zen Golf

CROW DOG PRESS
TURLOCK CA USA

The Grand Canyon Zen Golf Tour

A Memoir by Jack Random

Featuring
The Handbook of Zen Golf

Published by
Crow Dog Press
1241 Windsor Court
Turlock CA 95380

Copyright 2016 Ray Miller

All rights reserved. No part of this book may be reproduced in any form or by any means, electronic or mechanical, including photocopying, recording, or by any information storage and retrieval system, without permission in writing from the publisher.

Cover art by Artis Brown Miller.

ISBN-13: 978-0692605103
ISBN-10: 069260510X

THE GRAND CANYON ZEN GOLF TOUR

*May the journey be rich with experience
Imbued with inspiration
May it lead you to light
Infuse you with passion
And bless you with wisdom*

*May the journey inject your soul
With the spirit of adventure
Enlightenment and mystery*

*May the journey live forever in your heart
May your life be but a passage
In the journey of your soul*

And may the journey never end…

PREFACE

In the summer of 1993 I embarked on a cross-country journey from Nashville to California with a good friend and partner in jazz poetry. He has since undergone many incarnations but at the time I knew him as Wiz. Wiz was and is an extraordinary musician and craftsman. I had engaged him in a project to produce a jazz poetry play: *D'Arc Underground – A Jazz Play in Sixteen Choruses*. It retold the story of Joan of Arc with an invented language and a jazz background. Along with local poet Joe Speers and professional actress and musician Rhonda Coullet, we managed to record a version that Wiz converted into a stack of compact discs for distribution to the masses.

It was a pivotal time in my life. I was looking for change. I was reading Castaneda, Kerouac and Joseph Campbell, searching for spiritual grounding. I moved from California to Nashville to marry and support a woman in her struggle to succeed as a singer-songwriter. I met Wiz when we attended a coming-home party for folk hero John Prine. Wiz introduced himself and wanted to know if I was a jazz musician. I told him I was not. I was a playwright (at that time my writing focused on plays) but as it happened I was thinking about writing a jazz poetry play.

So began our association, our partnership and friendship. Wiz introduced me to the world of performance poetry and I introduced him to the game of golf – more specifically, Zen golf.

When I made plans to drive my 1965 Mustang to my family home in California that summer, Wiz asked to go with me and I agreed. What would have been a solitary journey filled with quiet reflection soon took on a more adventurous nature. We had our golf clubs. Wiz had his flute and I had my trumpet along with a portfolio of jazz poetry. We were determined to hit poetry venues, perform on the streets, and play golf at random points along the way.

Wiz spoke of the miraculous transformative powers of Grand Canyon so we added that to our list of destinations.

Much has transpired in the three decades since the journey chronicled here. I am happily remarried and living in California. Wiz lives a world apart at last notice on the panhandle of Florida. We both continue to pursue our artistic callings but we are not often in touch. Time and circumstance have moved us apart.

Still, the road trip in the summer of 1993 lives on in my memory and I trust in his as well. It had a dramatic impact on my life. It compelled me to look at the world with new eyes and reinforced my calling as an artist.

In the after word of this work, I have included *The Handbook of Zen Golf* – a work that Wiz and I brainstormed on the journey, along with a log of our gas and golf stops along the way. I decided against including *D'Arc Underground*, *Tales from Jazztown* or *Random Erotica*, works that also sprang from this journey or at least this time frame. Maybe they'll eventually find their own way into print.

The graphics in *The Grand Canyon Zen Golf Tour* and *The Handbook of Zen Golf* were created on the original Mac Paint program on the original 132K Mac. They are admittedly low tech and crude but I believe they capture the essence of their depictions.

As I read the original manuscript many years later, the words and the thoughts behind them seem almost hopelessly idealistic, even naïve. It represents a place in time when all things seemed possible. We existed as if on a separate plain where politics and war and terrorism did not exist. We were free to live in the moment and explore the mystical side of our selves.

For the record, the journey never ends.

CONTENTS

1.	Nashville Farewell	13
2.	The Crow	15
3.	Albuquerque	20
4.	Grand Canyon	31
5.	Three Rounds on The Road	39
6.	The Loneliest Road in America	48
7.	Flight of the Grey Eagle	52
8.	Down Home in The Valley	63
9.	Motown	67
10.	Golf at the Old Muni	74
11.	Shadow of Death	88
12.	Bay Area Poetry Scene	96
13.	Family Gathering	107
14.	Yosemite National Park	117
15.	Tioga Pass	125
16.	Sky of a Million Stars	134
17.	Boulder, Colorado	146
18.	Kansas Highway Blues	169
19.	The Heartland	180
20.	St. Louis and the Great Flood	185
21.	The Road Home to Nashville	192
22.	The Journey's End	197
23.	Homeless Angel	203
24.	The Journey Continues	209
25.	Post Script	213
26.	Appendix 1: Zen Golf Tour	215
27.	Appendix 2: Sally's Mileage	217
28.	The Handbook of Zen Golf	219

Zen Golf Editor's Note	221
Introduction	225
Lesson One: Balance	229
Lesson Two: Smooth & Easy	230
Lesson Three: Visualize the Shot	233
Lesson Four: It's Not the Score	234
Lesson Five: Enjoy the View	237
Lesson Six: Find the Center	238
Lesson Seven: Creative Impulse	239
Lesson Eight: Feel the All Force	240
Lesson Nine: Read the Signs	241
Lesson Ten: Pure Thoughts	242
Lesson Eleven: Relaxation is Key	243
Lesson Twelve: The Infinite Round	244
Lesson Thirteen: Praise the Gods	245
Lesson Fourteen: The Lesson of the Round	246
Lesson Fifteen: Welcome Adversity	247
Lesson Sixteen: Embrace the Simple	248
Lesson Seventeen: The Garden of Earth	249
Lesson Eighteen: Clear your Mind	250

ILLUSTRATIONS

Sacred Shot	35
Canyon Crow	38
Loneliest Road in America	47
Shadow of Death	92
Sky of a Million Stars	136
Esmeralda on the Streets of Boulder	153
Zen Golf Cover	223
Balance like a Scale	227
The Shot: Sit for a Hundred Years	231
Pacific Grove: Golf in The Kingdom	235

1

NASHVILLE FAREWELL

    Nashville, city of music, city of dreams, city of ambition and heartbreak, city of sweltering summers, lurid thunderstorms and enchanting fireflies, city of suddenly changing seasons, land of the Choctaw, Chickasaw, Shawnee and Cherokee, where the Civil War is living history and the rebel cry is still heard on back country roads, city of southern culture and racial strife, city of deafening cicada, red-winged blackbirds, ticks and chiggers, city of palatial mansions and southern charm, river city and land of endless forests, city of limestone and rock mountains, city of poverty, segregation and homelessness, city that seems to stand still in the eye of a hurricane, we bid you adieu.

    Though we strive to banish you from our minds for the length of the journey, we will hold you in our hearts, knowing that we will return to you reborn. Like wayward children we will welcome your familiar arms and you, unmoved, will acknowledge our passing. We are but falling leaves in an immense forest while you are the trees. We are the pilgrims in a land of adversity while you are the sanctuary. Whether you remain home to us or become a chapter in the history of our small, inconsequential lives, we will think of you often. But for now we must say So Long. We turn our backs and embark once more on the journey to uncover our souls, our dreams and our true natures.

Until we meet again: Farewell.

2

THE CROW

A large crow touches down in the middle of a busy highway and takes flight as we approach. It is a sign. Wait a thousand years and you will never see that sight again. The crow has chosen to be our guardian and guide on this journey. We welcome him and will look for him wherever the road takes us.

We are anxious, brimming with raw energy, and wish only to heed the signs and yield to our inner calling. We are seekers. We are warriors of the rolling highway. We are brothers by our own choosing and we have chosen to share the path of this sacred adventure. We do not know if our paths will part. The journey is a test of our kinship and we welcome it.

We have shared the Zen of the royal and ancient game of golf, the game of masters and the chess of sport. We are the jazz poets of the Nashville fringe. He is the wizard of the jazz poetry happening. He is the holder of the sacred flute. I am the writer of dreams.

We share a vision of the Grand Canyon and an enchanted shot under a full moon. We share the memories of journeys past. We are veterans of the dotted line who have roamed the interstates, highways and byways in search of life's illusive meaning. We are seekers of brotherhood and illumination.

We have gathered what knowledge and wisdom we could from the words of Siddhartha, Zen and The Art of Motorcycle Maintenance, Dharma Bums, On the Road, Don Juan and Journey to Ixtlan. We have traveled in peyote dreams. We have seen the desert through the eyes of the coyote. We have ridden the wind of a Pacific sunset. We have reserved a place in our hearts and minds for people and locations past and present. We hold to them like treasures of the soul and wish to breathe into them new, eternal life.

We leave behind our loves and the mystery of how they will receive us on our return. For now and for the length of the journey we are creatures of the universe. We are open and free. We hunger for adventure. We are eager to greet our common or separate destinies.

For myself it is a journey home as well as away from home. It has only been a year since I married and left California. Only a year, twelve ticks on the calendar, and yet it seems profound. My life has changed and my heart is divided. I sense the unsettling of my soul has something to do with letting go. But how do I let go of friends and family that have been so great a part of all that I am and all that I value? How do I let go without letting go? Somehow I must find an answer.

We shoot like a blast of tequila out of Nashville and into the receding sun. The great expansive forest land of Tennessee, the city of Memphis and the bulging Mississippi, the rolling hills and dales of Arkansas and Oklahoma blur like a distant memory.

Rolling through the Texas panhandle in a sunny blaze, Wiz decides to take action. The process of Mustang Sally's preparation for the journey included replacing the gas tank. It had rusted in the tropical air of Tennessee. I didn't notice that the spare tire was missing until departure day. Too late. Aside from the time factor, the place had gone out of business. I'm willing to risk it but Wiz is wary about crossing the desert without one. I know he's right.

He spots what he thinks is a promising side road that leads us to an unaffiliated gas station. Wiz connects with the good old boys whose game of checkers we've interrupted. They try on three different tires without success and refer us to a junkyard down the road. We locate the place and walk in.

There seems to be some confusion about whose job it is to deal with the intruders. It's a family operation. In the small office space there are three generations of transplanted southerners – people from the Deep South, Louisiana, Georgia, Mississippi and such. Wiz draws on his Alabama upbringing and makes inquiry about the spare. It sits a while until the right man shows up in the office.

"Sixty-five Mustang. Right."

He takes off to search for the tire and rim while we sit back and wait. One by one the members of the family raise their heads from whatever occupies them to give us a look. The youngest of three children playing in the office, whose name is Bubba or Spanky or something akin, approaches Wiz and demands: Get out of my chair! Wiz is dumbfounded, throws up his hands and rises to find another place to sit.

I make eye contact with the kid, sitting in *his* chair, and we share a good laugh. It breaks the spell. We are accepted into their circle. Smiles all around. All is well. The change in atmosphere allows us to look around. The walls are covered with old black-and-white photographs depicting black people in a curious mixture with white folks. Good old boys. The blacks have large smiles and are generally the center of focus while the whites linger at the sides or in the background, seeming pleased and proud.

I realize later that the blacks are in servitude, whether slaves or hired servants I do not know. The confirmation comes outside where Wiz helps the guy try on the spare. We get a real good deal and say So Long. As we're driving away Wiz points a finger at a bumper sticker on the rear window of the family pickup. It reads: White Empire. It has a reference to God's Country.

I know this phenomenon knows no geographical boundaries. There are white supremacy strongholds in central California and the Great Northwest. Still, my own upbringing does not allow me to feel comfortable in these settings. Maybe it's the respect I have for the blacks I grew up with. Maybe it's the memory of Ben May, an African-American classmate who stood up for a group of white boys when we were surrounded by an angry black mob on the Westside of Modesto during the race riots of the Watts era. Maybe it's the Apache blood that runs through my veins [1] or the high regard I have for the Native American spirit.

Whatever it is, I am uncomfortably grateful I did not put it together until now. I'm not good at hiding my feelings despite years of acting experience. To the people of the White Empire at a north Texas junkyard we were good old boys with a healthy sense of humor. To us they are the white supremacists that gave us a fair deal on the Texas panhandle. It is something I will ponder when there is time for reflection. Right now there is no time. We're on the road. Our eyes are fixed dead ahead, on the line to the next destination.

We emerge, as if from a long dark tunnel, on the

high desert plains, a land of red rock monuments and an endless road that shoots across a horizon of blood red and purple shadow to the oasis city of Albuquerque, New Mexico. Here we will rest, collect our thoughts, breathe deeply the spirit of the crow and the desert air. Here we will encounter whatever awaits us on the first official destination of the journey.

[1] A Mormon family member reported that very summer that my great grandmother on my father's side was a full-blood Apache. That discovery has since been questioned.

3

ALBUQUERQUE

Albuquerque was once a chosen stop on *The Hitchhiker's Guide to the College of Your Choice*. That reference and the fact that The Beatlicks, Joe and Pamela Speer, the royal couple of the Nashville poetry scene, hail from Albuquerque, pulls us here now.

In many ways we form an odd partnership. Wiz combines the characteristics of a Zen master and an extraordinary musician with the sensibilities and attitudes of the southern culture. He has a gift for connecting to people while I tend to pull back and observe from an objective distance.

For all our differences and incongruities we are the same in one essential way: We are seekers of secret knowledge and divine wisdom. Our path led us here for a reason and we were determined to find it.

On Route 66, Albuquerque is one of those towns where the old VW busses broke down on the westward journey to the People's Revolution on the California coast – LA, Berkeley, San Francisco and Monterey. Rather than press their luck with a desert crossing, they staged their own cultural revolution here. It was a stop that somehow eluded us both on our previous travels.

Driving into town I am struck by an uneasy feeling. Had there been some mistake? What kind of town is this? The outskirts have all the markings of fleeting resolve, like a temporary encampment: Tin can shelters on the slopes of desert mountains, trailer camps, junkyards and tacky little shops set up for business. Were these the dwellings of city Indians or aging hippies surviving on the fringe, still waiting for a few parts and a little more mechanical tinkering before pushing on to the coast?

From the eastside the closer you get to the University of New Mexico, a metamorphosis takes hold. Tie-dye shirts and head shops appear. We hear the beat of bongos and congas on the streets. Coolness hangs out in the local cafes listening to folk music and open mike poetry readings. Peace symbols and rainbows are everywhere.

The people here don't know what to make of the Nashville jazz poets. Comfortable in their coolness they invite no impetus for change. We take the stage at a poetry cafe.

Jazzman on the corner of the Frontier Restaurant
Blowing cool breeze into the dry New Mexico heat
Faces drop eyes wide open like a spaceship
Landing in the courtyard

Jazz poetry in the local hip-hop café
Like a stone in black water
Dissolves without a trace

They'd rather hear Cat Stevens'
Oh very young what will you leave us this time?

Poetry is dead. Long live poetry.

Wild man on the streets
Strikes terror in the hearts of peacenik poets
Fuck peace! Peace to you! he cries
As peacenik poets avert their eyes

Fat tire bike cops in khaki shorts
Sun bathed bronze amber vision shades
Talk him down with peace love and
Brother be not proud!

They send him on his way and take their bows
To the admiring poets of a sidewalk café

The wild man re-emerges from the shadows
Walks into the night alone

He is Bukowski, madman poet of the lost & forlorn
Banned on the streets of Albuquerque

Poetry is dead. Long live poetry.

In two days we play rounds of nine on three different courses. Our fellow golfers are easy and eager to engage. They speak of places and layouts and offer advice. We find our comfort and play with ease.

The courses strike a contrast. The University North layout is lined with trees with doglegs left and right. The greens are small and slow, matching the pace of play. A nine-hole course next to the airport is windswept and hilly. A sign on the first tees warns players not to hit aircraft.

The University South course is booked so we're forced to play a three-hole beginner course. It is the most enlightening. We circle it three times while we observe the progress of a Zen golf lesson each time we make a pass. The driving range is between the third green and the first tee. On the first pass the master, a middle-aged woman with an air of grace, speaks of finding your center. By the last pass the master is gone and the student is hitting balls from a one-legged stance. As she slowly takes the club back, she raises her left foot, methodically shifts her knee to center and replants her foot as she strikes the ball.

It is a phenomenon of infinite beauty. Golf from the solar plexus. Balance is the first lesson. Without balance all other lessons are unnecessary. As with golf so it is with life.

In the evening I accompany Wiz's free flowing flute with jazz poetry on the streets. We gather a small following of young tie-dyes, children of the late sixties. They seem to gaze at us with a measure of wonder and awe. They have a mixture of respect and doubt. My words have bite. We carry more than a pleasant breeze and dharmic overtures. We infuse our message with irony, cynicism, fire and rebellion.

They pay us tribute in their quiet way and distance themselves in caution. We move on to the poetry café and place our names on the list. We order cappuccinos and wait.

The poetry reminds me of television soap and Oprah Winfrey: Open heart confessionals, political diatribes tuned to the audience and thoughts while walking under the full moon of a desert landscape.

The emcee makes a joke about playing war as a child. Precision bombing is such a treat. He begins an Indian chant accompanied by guitar. I hear drums in the distance, drowning the messenger with discord. This is sacred land. The white man may settle here for a thousand years but the Indian will still own the land and the coyote will dance on his grave.

The poet's satisfied smile belies his message. He speaks of his wild days, Jack Daniels and Harley Davidson, leather, tattoos and blowin' in the wind as if they laid out his living resume. He finds comfort and security as emcee of the local poetry café.

The poets make their way to the exit as we take the stage. I announce the death of poetry and wonder aloud why the *real* poets hurry to depart before their own words have settled with the lattes and pastries. Again I think of Bukowski. We have their attention. The exodus freezes. Wiz rails on the resident piano (Bukowski: Play the Piano Drunk Like a Percussion Instrument until the Fingers Begin to Bleed a Bit) and I begin:

We are the scum that crawls out of the cracks
in America's nightmare
We are the byproducts of industrial wastelands
We are the residue of filthy minds
We are the dregs of technologic crime…

I realize midway that we have become my words in the eyes of our audience. We have delivered a shock to their system and they do not like it. They sense their unity of purpose under attack and the barriers of defense rise up yet they listen intently despite themselves. They deliver a sincere and vigorous applause at the end of our performance and the evening comes to a close.

We have made an impact but the effect is not what we might have hoped. Back in Nashville guest artists in the poetry scene would at the least be invited for drinks or a smoke. That is not happening here. We are the outcasts. Even our curious young followers have abandoned us. We are untouchable. We are the new wild men of the streets on the Albuquerque scene. We are the destroyers, the terrorists, the anarchists and we are not to be welcomed in the fold. Like the wild man of Albuquerque they will not look us in the eyes.

   A part of me wonders if we have chosen the wrong path. If I put myself in their shoes, would I react differently? No one likes outsiders coming in to tell you how to think, how to write or what to do with your performance poetry venue. I hope I would welcome the challenge and engage the challengers but would I do so without resentment, without pushing back or avoiding contact? I do not know.

   We are committed as artists to being agents of change. We do wish to destroy the art of comfort, the poetry of passivity, the circles of poets that exist only to applaud their own creativity without ever reaching out to the greater world. We sound a discordant note to awaken a new and deeper meaning as a purpose for our artistic endeavors. Should we be content with poets reading to poets while the extended family of humanity remains outside, unmoved and untouched? Of all people shouldn't poets understand and embrace the death of poetry for only with death can poetry be reborn?

   We have succeeded in our mission to shake things up. They will remember what we have done here long after we are gone. Some of these same poets may be inspired to write and perform more challenging and less comfortable works. If so they will engage with eyes open, knowing there is a price. They may be pushed away from the fold. They may become the wild man on the streets: Peace to you!

After a spell a poet walks up to compliment our multimedia approach and advises us to show up earlier in the evening next time. Wiz and I glance at each other. We know there will not be a next time. The man shuffles and fidgets and folds back into his circle. Maybe he's afraid to be seen in communion with the outcasts. Maybe he's just uncomfortable. He will be here tomorrow. We will not.

Peace to you!

The reading charges our batteries. We are not ready to call it a night. We feel anxious and unfulfilled. We need more stimulation. A waitress at the poetry café recommends a downtown nightclub so we set out on foot, cross the tracks and enter the old district. It is the wild side of Albuquerque, populated by resident punks, hippies, bums, leathers, pimps, whores and drag queens.

We walk up to a burrito stand advertising health foods. An attractive blonde working the stand explains that her burritos are lard free. We're impressed and order a couple. We hang out and gather her story.

She looks like she belongs at Venice Beach in southern California rather than on the wild side of Albuquerque selling healthy burritos. She has a genuine friendliness, a free spirit manner about her and an appearance that would draw gazes at Cannes. It turns out she has a degree in accounting. She came to Albuquerque to help her father with his business but they couldn't get along so now she was in transition.

We ask her what's happening and she gives us a rundown on the bar scene. She says they used to have a hip-hop night but it drew too many guns. We take that as a warning. There be danger here. New Mexico law allows a person to carry a gun into a bar as long as it's visible. I can't figure why hip-hop as opposed to hard rock or country attracted too many guns but I let it pass. We decide to step in for a beer and thank her for the dialogue. She smiles and wishes us well. She means it. We don't take it as an invitation. It belongs to the world and she offers it freely to everyone she encounters.

There is a three-dollar cover that applies to three bars in the neighborhood. We pay and go inside. The club is divided into three sections. One has a three-piece punk band on an elevated platform with a video backdrop. The crowd is young, hip and the place is packed, standing room only. In the back room an elevated disc jockey plays electronic punk and controls lighting effects on a small crowded dance floor. Upstairs there is a small bar with sofas and padded chairs. The crowd is sparse and the space is quiet enough for conversation.

We sit down, take a load off and drink our beers while gazing out on the dance floor below. We talk about the age barrier, the passage of time and the distance between us and our lives in Nashville. We take note of the women in the joint. Unlike myself, Wiz is theoretically free of obligation but his sense of loyalty remains intact. Though we are willing to enjoy the pull and temptation of attraction we are not willing to cross the line.

We walk out and wander down the street looking for a jazz club, offer a couple of bucks to two Indians with a shopping cart full of junk and spot a happening club with a big crowd mixing it up in good spirits. Wiz spots what appears to be a Latina fox in a sexy black dress and identifies her for what she is: a man. It's a drag joint with a good number of attractive women shaking it up with queens outside. One of them gives me a look that sends a charge through my libido. Inside it looks like a bad production of *Pink Flamingos*. We walk on.

The time has come to leave this town. No regrets. The lessons delivered will take time to gather and comprehend. The decidedly conflicted reception by the poetry community weighs heavy on our minds. Like the wild man of the streets, maybe the most misunderstood individual in town, there must be a better way. If we look in the right places, we'll find it.

Poetry like golf is not important in itself. But poetry is important to us here and now and like so many things in life that traditionally offer comfort and maybe some sense of meaning in a world of chaos, it is in great danger of ceasing to exist. It is infected with the deadly disease of boredom. Traditional art forms must evolve or die. Then let her die gracefully, in comfort or in rage, for with death comes the promise of evolution.

That is the hope of poetry and the role of the poet is to shape the living poetry of the future. It is already happening. It is being incorporated, as Dylan once projected, in music. We should not be too quick to judge rap or hip-hop or any other form of creative expression. All forms are valid. All messages are signs that will be read by intended eyes. All messengers are children of god, creatures of light and carriers of the sacred flame. We should listen most intently to those who disrupt our vision for there is the message that will expand our view and guide us forward.

For now we choose to remember Albuquerque mostly for the golf. Balance is the first lesson. We will not stray from the path that chooses us. We will find our center and hold on to it as an infant clings to her mother's breast.

To Albuquerque we give our blessing:
Peace to you.

Streaking across the desert skyline
Albuquerque to Grand Canyon in a heartbeat
Coasting on the fumes of yesterday's drive
The dream alive by a thin white line

Riding the high plains under moonlight
Fleeting glimpse of higher truths
Spoken in tongues delivered in codes
Visible only beyond our sight

4

GRAND CANYON

Sacred shot into the bottomless void
The grandeur of humility
The infinity of small
Freedom soars on the wings of angels
Ride the winds of endless time
Only the gods can see the whole
Only mother earth can hold its sanctity
We are children even in our greatest wisdom

The sun dissolves with an orange and purple glow as we make our way to the earth's great divide. We have crossed endless miles of Indian reservations.

We attempted and failed to score mescal. We forgot they do not allow the selling of alcohol on reservation land. We forget the once proud tribes are still ruled by the foreign invaders. We forget that these are a conquered people, still protected from the weakness that the white man used to defeat them.

It is a strange phenomenon to see Quik Stops and Exxon stations, the golden arches and Super 8 motels, and to be reminded that this is the last resting ground of the Navaho. We have traversed the land of the Zuni and the Petrified Forest. We have traveled the land of the Apache and the Painted Desert.

A medicine woman's spell still lingers in the warm dry air, her weathered face etched in primordial terrain. A sacred dance is still performed on the mesa in a circle of red rock mountains. The shadow of an ancient shaman still hovers above us in the evening sky. A lonely coyote yaps and sends us on our way. The crow is always with us. No mescal. No tequila. No alcohol. We are on our own.

We decide against a detour to Grey Mountain, a town just outside the reservation that sells plenty of fire water, and race the fading sunlight to this day's destiny: Grand Canyon.

We witness along the way, in two-by-four shelters draped with canvas and plastic tarps, the new Indians, the commercial Indians, Manhattan's revenge. A sign proclaims them "friendly" Indians. They sell jewelry, authentic Indian jewelry, handcrafted silver and turquoise necklaces, rings, medicine pouches and jade earrings.

The sun hovers in a brilliant amber glow. We have lost the race and pull over to a trace canyon, a small sliver of the Grand. The merchant Indians, packing their wares, give us a glance and sense that we are neither buyers nor a threat to their welfare. They allow us to pass unobstructed to the edge of their little canyon.

I am dumbstruck and sit to ponder the hand of god. Wiz is less impressed. He has been to the Grand. He has walked her ledge and camped on her floor while my eyes are virgin to this awe. I am aware of the great glaciers that cut and shaped Yosemite Valley but this a different creature with a distinctly different spiritual sensation. In a part of the world that desperately needed shelter it is as if the earth opened her womb and gave birth to the greatest shelter the world has ever known. A microcosm world of its own, a world of such depth and breadth it challenges the eye and questions the very meaning of existence. It invokes flight of mind and humbles the most confident of men.

We move on to the Grand and savor the remaining moments of twilight as we make our way to the edge of the abyss. Here, under the light of a full moon, I catch my first glimpse of the unfathomable. The name itself summons mythology. Was it here beneath the infinite stars of heaven that Prometheus descended with the flame of human enlightenment? Was it here that the muses entertained the gods with music, dance and poetry? Was it here that Hades abducted Persephone and carried her into the bowels of the earth?

We stop briefly at the first lookout. Towering mountains, cliffs, valleys and bluffs encapture this slice of earth so far below that the mind cannot grasp its reality. Chasms within chasms. Another world, separate and distinct. A monument to all forces greater than humanity. Its vastness is beyond the realm of imagination yet I am struck by the feeling that I have seen this sight before. Another life, a dream, a crystal meditation? Here on this holy spot of earth all things are possible.

It's late. We have to find our place along the canyon ledge before nightfall and before the park ranger discovers us. Wiz spots an overnight parking lot for hikers at the second lookout and we pull over. I stay with Sally while he scrambles for a place to plant our things out of the sight of rangers.

When he returns we quickly unload: Sleeping bags, small packs, a couple of beers, two golf balls, two tees and a single five iron. We scramble down to the chosen spot. It is a small granite ledge just below and to the left of the lookout. It is truly majestic. The canyon branches to our left and opens in all its glory before us. The mountains springing from the canyon floor split into three chasms: One toward the north rim, another branches to the east and a third to the west below us.

A mist begins to gather in the chasms of the canyon floor as we explore our surroundings for alternate points of view. Our exploration confirms that we have chosen well by intuition – or rather it has chosen us. We return to our spot and settle in for the show. This is the only place we have found where a golf tee can be planted.

I tee up my ball and carefully clean the path of the swing. As I test the address position I find two imprints in the granite ledge that perfectly fit the soles of my moccasins. All doubt removed: This is the spot. Like Castaneda rolling around on the porch of Don Juan, Wiz has tapped the greater forces to locate our place. It is not only the best spot; it is the only spot. If we had not found it our destiny would surely have been altered.

One does not slap or punch a ball into Grand Canyon. To do so would be a sacrilege, an affront not only to the canyon but to the game that has come to symbolize so much in our lives.

I plant my moccasins in the indentations on the ledge and rehearse the swing with great care. I am aware that the force of a golf swing can propel the golfer in any direction, including forward. Just as one does not speak of water on a water hole or out-of-bounds right on a long par four, I dare not speak this thought aloud. Often speaking of doubt creates doubt and envisioning misfortune enhances the probability of such an outcome. In the world of golf Wiz is my student. I prepare myself. I will teach by example only, by the sincerity and thoughtfulness I devote to it. There will be no second chance.

Satisfied, I lay the club along the line where the toes of my feet will be in my stance. Then I sit and wait for the moment. Again and again I visualize the shot. I see the backswing, the rotation of the body, the uncoiling and the flight of the ball in the depths. I free my mind of all other thoughts, focus on my center and wait.

Finally, as the mist rises in the canyon below, I see the white of the ball glowing as if from inner illumination. The light of the moon springs through the overhanging shrubs and bushes, shining a sacred triangle on the ball.

I rise, take up the club, plant my feet, address the ball and suddenly, as if some external force has claimed control of my inner being, I begin the swing. Like a pendulum the club head starts its backward motion, my left shoulder pivots downward below my chin, weight shifts inward toward my right knee and hip, wrists cock at the top of the swing, my hands spring forward as the weight of my body follows closely behind to the point of impact. The coil is unleashed. The club head, still on its downward plane, strikes the ball squarely, snapping the white tee crisply into two equal halves. My body squares to the target of the canyon as the club completes the cycle of its own momentum. My feet remain planted.

The ball disappears on contact: A sacred shot into the largest hole on the planet. It is my first hole-in-one.

As Wiz tees up his Hogan and takes his address, we do not mention that it is indeed possible to miss. His preparation is not as long but no less sincere. His swing is full, powerful and fearless. He draws sparks from the granite a fraction behind the ball, a clear sign of contact on a downward plane. Again the ball disappears on impact. Another ace.

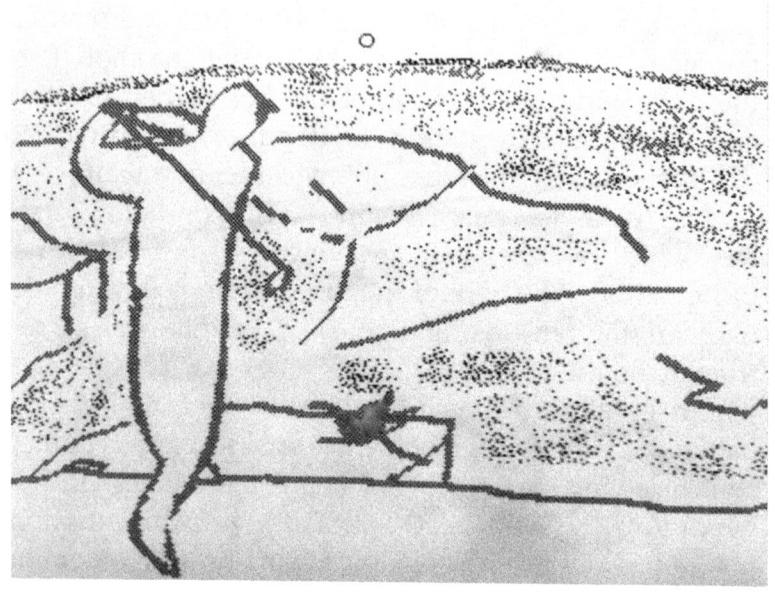

We have succeeded in this mission more gloriously than we could have imagined. We sit back to reflect and bask in the splendor of the moment.

Exhaustion overtakes us. We talk a while and witness the expected visit of the park ranger on the bluff above (he does not discover us). Then we climb in our bags and let sleep envelope us with dreams of other worlds, other dimensions and separate realities.

We awaken several times during the course of the night and witness startling changes in the canyon. It fills with mist until the clouds below are joined with clouds in the sky above. A more mystical vision cannot be observed in the physical realm.

I wonder if Wiz is struck by the same curious desire to jump into the void – curious in that it is by no means a death wish. It is the suspended belief that we are spiritual entities capable of walking to the stars. I have felt the same sensation driving down Highway One on the northern California coast during sunset. It is a sense of being outside oneself and somehow beyond the hold of gravity.

When I next awaken it is morning. Wiz is off exploring and I find my sleeping bag has slid down the ledge, leaving my legs dangling over the abyss. It is time to rise.

I stare at the site of the sacred golf shots for some time before I pack my things in the car and hunt down Wiz to join his exploration. Tourists have begun to arrive. A German couple seems shy, perhaps humbled by the canyon. A Japanese man and woman share youthful smiles. The man lets loose a blood curdling yell. He cannot contain his joy.

Before we leave our sacred place, a spot the tourists do not discover, two large crows rise up from the canyon to greet us and send us on our way. One settles on a bush directly in front of us, scans the canyon and then peers into the space behind my eyes. It is said that if you look into the eyes of the crow you are allowed to see the future. I am filled with calm and wonder.

We stop once more to see an Indian dwelling, a round stone tower with nonlinear openings – perhaps lookouts to observe approaching enemies. It has been rebuilt and fashioned as a gift shop. The day is too young for it to be open but already the tourists are gathering: more Germans, Japanese and French nationals with cameras and wide-eyed curiosity. Ironically, there are more foreigners at Grand Canyon than Americans.

Why is it that we never fully appreciate the beauty and majesty in our own back yards?

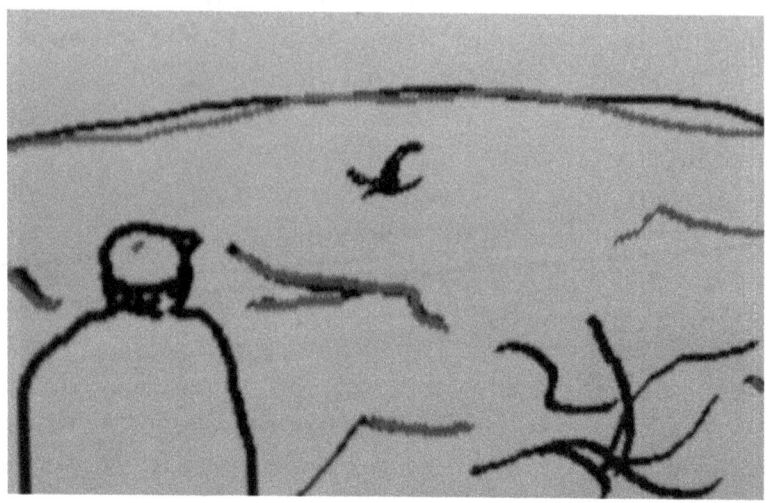

We leave Grand Canyon the way we came, east and north through the reservation. Strangely, the park station is unmanned. We are allowed to come and go without charge. This is the way it should be. I deposit a ten-dollar bill below the floor mat. There it will remain until needed.

5

THREE ROUNDS ON THE ROAD

We stop in Page, Arizona, by Lake Powell, a creation of the Glen Canyon Dam on the Colorado River. Wiz remembers this place as the best swimming hole in the west. With sincere passion he describes translucent shades of blue and green and a sparkling clarity born of the mile-deep waters. It conjures memories of Crater Lake in Oregon.

Inevitably the congenial grey-haired lady at the combination gas station and convenience store tells us about the local golf course and our day is set. It is a flat nine-holer with wide, tree-lined fairways, water hazards and rabbits by the score.

We play with the theme of inner self. I sink a forty-foot putt for birdie and finish two over par. Wiz beats fifty for the fourth time since taking up the game in earnest only a month ago. We both make shots with a five iron that allow us to imagine what our shots in to the great moonlit void might have looked like had we been able to see the flight of the ball.

We have a good meal at the clubhouse where the bartender speaks of sexism at the dam. She has a degree in engineering and took a job here fresh out of college. Being female and a recent college graduate, the men under her authority seemed to resent her. Being smaller than the men she was frequently called on to crawl into small spaces. On one such occasion the men locked the door behind her. A lawsuit followed. The men responsible were fired but she ended up quitting.

She stayed on in Page as a bartender, a good position she implies to keep watch and have her revenge on the men who stray from common decency or the obligations of marriage. We wish each other well and she notes that they have a band at night should we still be in town.

The swimming hole is a water-filled rock canyon next to the dam. The water is brilliant and clear but Wiz sees a thin sheath of gasoline from powerboats. In only a year humans have marked these pristine waters with toxins. Imagine what will happen in ten years. How frail the beauty of nature now seems next to the impregnable grandeur of Grand Canyon. Like graffiti on the wall of El Capitan in Yosemite, some people just cannot resist leaving their mark. I now understand why boating and recreation have come under fire at Crater Lake and Lake Tahoe.

I remember seeing where humans had chipped away at a crystal waterfall in a California cave called the Crystal Palace. I remember thinking: How could anyone be so insensitive?

Nature's wonders must be protected even from their human admirers. One minute of damage may take a hundred years to repair. It is the worst of human instinct to want to own or mark nature in one way or another.

We had discussed our shots into the canyon and wondered if it could be considered littering. I think not. For the golf ball, pure as snow, is a sacred object. Had we fired a dozen range balls into the canyon that would be littering but a single shot under a full moon, the mists of heaven and earth converging, was nothing more and nothing less than a sacred offering.

Wiz sends out some inspired music as an offering of peace and healing to mother earth. Perhaps it will help. Maybe it will calm an angry man or inspire a young child. It strikes me now as odd he did not choose to play at Grand Canyon. Maybe he was overwhelmed by its perfection. Maybe its magnitude was too great for accompaniment. I never thought to ask but the answer is simple: the impulse did not strike.

Once again we are on the road. Our bodies are rested and our spirits soar though we have not slept long. The spirit of the crow goes with us and its strength is more powerful now than ever. The force that guides us all pulls us to our destiny and we do not resist.

We head north and cross into Utah. We are at a crossroad on the journey. Our senses sharpened, our awareness heightened, we fight against anticipation but there exists an undeniable eagerness in our spirits.

Golf has become prominent in our minds. We carry two books: Bukowski and *Golf in The Kingdom* by Michael Murphy. Perhaps the greatest Zen Golf book every written, we open it at random on a daily basis and follow its decree. A tradition born in Albuquerque, on one occasion Wiz decided it might be a good time to rent an electric cart. The daily lesson read something like this: It is not the shot; it is the walk. Needless to say we did not rent a cart and would not for the remainder of our journey.

We have begun taking notes for *A Pocketbook of Zen Golf*. Its lessons are as varied as the game itself and the geography on which it is played.

Balance is the first lesson. Without balance there is nothing. Julius Boros: The swing's the thing. Find the center. Be the trees. See the flight of the ball before the shot. Be the ball. Clear the mind. Welcome adversity. Any shot that can be imagined can be made. Approach the game with humility. Julius Boros: Swing easy, hit hard. Be the wind. Let the club select you. Golf is a game of opposites. Breathe. The path of the club, the flight of the ball, the grass, the sand, the trees, the birds, wildlife, butterflies, the air, the running water and the rustling leaves: Everything around you and within you is one.

By the time we reach Zion National Park we are primed and ready to receive the sign that now appears: A golf course on the roadside, laid out in a chiseled valley with red rock and clay formations, sculptures of mother earth above. It is mid-afternoon and hot. The wind whips across the course in waves of dry heat. Be the wind.

There are two ways to play the wind. One is to hit the ball straight and let the wind to move it to the target. The other is to hit a ball that curves into or with the current, thereby merging with the wind or opposing it. I favor the latter approach.

Wiz chides me on the first tee. Aware that people in the clubhouse are watching, he wonders aloud whether I am road weary. I hit what is known in golf as a wormer (a worm never leaves the ground). I have cautioned Wiz before to respect other golfers and honor the etiquette of the game. I have allowed him to chide me, however, believing that I should welcome the challenge of distractions.

It is a fine line. If you allow fellow golfers to engage in such practices (commonly known as gamesmanship) how are they to learn it is not acceptable behavior? I have come to the conclusion that it should only be necessary to inform a fellow player once or twice (not to talk while a golfer addresses the ball, not to step on a putting line, not to invade a golfer's space by standing behind the ball as the player putts or hits); after that there is no recourse but to find other playing partners.

Back in Nashville Wiz decided it would be funny to chant "Hey batter-batter...swing!" as I missed a birdie putt. To any golfer it was an egregious affront to the game. I waited for my anger to subside and informed him that he had about seven holes of bad karma to deal with. His game went into a tailspin. After three holes of atonement I handed him a tee and suggested he repair an unfixed ball mark on the green. He repaired several ball marks on the next two greens and his game returned to him. Lesson learned.

Wiz hits a solid drive and continues his harassment albeit in good spirits. My second shot sails while his hops along the ground like a squirrel looking for nuts. By the fourth hole we're both struggling. We are playing against the wind and against each other. We have become the Anti-Zen despite ourselves.

I raise my head and breathe in the beauty that surrounds us. This is truly one of the more beautiful desert links courses we will ever be blessed to play yet we, like spoiled children, wage war against each other, creating our own hell in paradise. Breathe. Smell the sweet desert air. Be the wind.

We begin to play golf. Good karma like bad is contagious. The ball sails and bends into the wind. We steer it with our minds. We talk to the ball in flight and it listens. At the seventh tee we are asked to play through by a family of beginning golfers. We greet them with smiles and protest that we are in no hurry but they insist. We hit drives worthy of Ben Hogan and Bobby Jones. Our balls have wings and soar like hawks with a force greater than our swings. We have found peace. We have become one with the game in all its glory. We finish the round and resume our journey on the same high with which we left Grand Canyon.

Thirty miles down the road we come across yet another course. Though the sun is descending in the western sky we do not hesitate. We accept this blessing and follow. A sign instructs us to pay for the round at the gas station and convenience store. The cost is three dollars per nine. A sign by the cash register notes that the last clerk was fired for giving away golf rounds. At that price he should have been and the golfers banned from the game. In this day and age three dollars a nine is a blessing not to be believed. Three dollars a nine would open the game to the world and the world would be better for it.

The course is short and features an imaginative layout. Children, ducks, swans and rabbits inhabit the course and the grass is almost supernaturally green. The scorecard reads: The greenest grass in Utah! The fairways are lined with birch trees with their distinctive white bark. We hear laughter and a pleasant breeze beneath the setting sun soothes us.

We tee off on a short par four and overshoot the green to the right. After a brief hunt Wiz locates his ball and lifts a wedge shot onto the green. We proceed to play some of the best golf of the journey.

By the time we climb to the elevated ninth tee we walk on air, a sense of elation and profound peace comforting our souls. The Zen of Golf. I am aware that Wiz is playing perhaps his best round ever.

We wait for the foursome ahead to play their second shots. The sun has nearly fallen from the sky. The sprinklers come on, charging the atmosphere with a pulse and a rhythm, like a spiritual pendulum. The air carries a golden glow. Everything around us seems to emanate a powerful force. We observe the flow of energy in the field of play.

I step to the tee and hit a solid shot that sails right into a gully. Wiz sends a rocket dead center. Not bad if you like perfect. We descend from the tee and walk down the fairway in triumph. Zen. Nirvana. We are more than brothers now. We are comrades. There is a bond and an implicit sense of trust between us in this moment of spiritual high that is unbreakable and beyond human understanding.

Wiz says, "Don Juan would be proud."

At that moment the sprinkler in front of us, guided by the hand of the master himself, alters its direction and sends a steady stream right at us. I bolt to the left and the water follows. I spring to the right and it stays with me. My momentum carries me full force into the waiting shoulder of Wiz and we explode in laughter.

Wiz says, "Don Juan is laughing at us."

We have the good sense to laugh at ourselves. We finish the hole in good humor. Wiz records his best score but it will be remembered as much, much more. We may tell ourselves and sincerely believe that we have found IT – the zone, the Zen, the core, nirvana, the truth, perfection – but we have not. The one sure thing is that those who have found IT have no need or desire to speak of it. It is a state of being that is in constant motion, changing, dissolving and transforming into something else.

We have only begun our journey. We have played

three rounds on the road in one day and still found time to bathe in the waters of the Colorado River. We are not tired. Like the ball with wings we are charged by a separate and greater source of strength. It radiates within and stimulates a hunger for the next adventure.

Wiz calls his parents from a payphone outside the gas station. It is their anniversary. He tells his father about his golf round and his score. His father replies with humor and a touch of doubt: "They're making you count them now, are they?"

We have a meal at the restaurant next door and I take note of a statement on the menu: They add a ten percent tip to the tab, explaining that 70% of their customers are Europeans and unaccustomed to American tipping.

This is Utah! Where I wonder are the Americans? Have we made our roads too dangerous for the young people who once traveled these highways in search of self and a greater understanding? Where are the working class retired folks in recreational vehicles and vans that once roamed this scenic landscape as a reward for their working lives? Have they discovered that the fruits of their labor, a life of saving and getting by, are inadequate to the purpose? Have they lost interest?

It is the second sign of this phenomenon I have seen on this journey and it leaves me wondering. The road used to be a place separate from society – almost immune to the changing times. A place to find truth and freedom, it was always worth the risk to explore the country and its disparate people. No more. Now it seems the road has become a desperate place that only foreigners explore. When did the American spirit of adventure slip away?

We decide against booking a motel room and choose instead to cross the barren Nevada desert in the cool of the night. The moon shines bright and we are charged with mystical energy. The High Sierras of California beckon us in the distance.

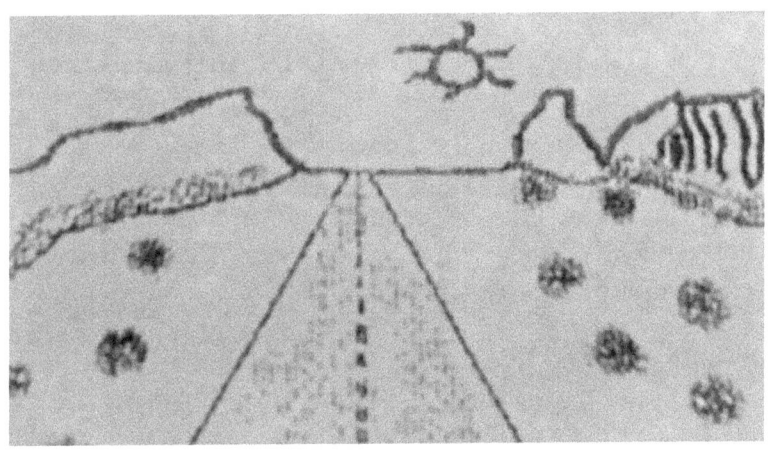

Ancient land of the Hopi
Sacred land of the Navaho
Chosen ground of the lone coyote
Cloudless sky of the crow
Barren land of the white man's waste
Where they dig for oil, platinum, uranium
As the natives are safely shoved aside
The loneliest road in America

6

THE LONELIEST ROAD IN AMERICA

It is officially proclaimed: The Loneliest Road in America – an endless stretch of flat desert highway between Ely and Fallon, Nevada. Ely is a major crossroad in this desolate land. Tourist attractions – such as they are – include casinos and one of the world's largest mining pits.

We are not ready to stop in Ely. We fill up Sally with gas and begin the desert crossing. It is flatland, barren yet the elevation ranges from six to seven thousand feet above sea level. There are no trees, no wires and no electrical lights to be seen. Nothing but sagebrush and an eerie sensation, death and foreboding, awaits us in the cool desolate air.

Wiz is at the wheel when we encounter Kamikaze rabbits. They dash across the highway and turn directly into Sally's headlights. This is a breed of animal behavior I have never before witnessed. I have seen animals of all kinds – deer, coyotes and possums – freeze in the lights of approaching vehicles and in their disorientation attempt to escape by breaking the wrong way, into the path of a moving car. But I have never seen an animal plunge so willingly into the center of a roaring beast.

It shudders my soul and sets my mind to worry and

wonder. What lies beyond our naked view here in this barren land that spurs such abhorrent behavior? There are thousands of them, far more than this desert can support. Have they arrived at this solution to overpopulation? Is this an evolutionary act of survival, an unnatural thinning of the herd or are there other forces at work here, chemicals or radiation that poison and torture the unfortunate of the species? Is this what it seems: a voluntary self-extermination?

As we drive along we witness a deer that startles us with a gesture that reminds us of the suicidal rabbits, striking fear that this creature will take us down with him. We see an antelope that watches us with seeming detachment and a lone coyote. The coyote alone seems at home in this place. Alone among mammals, the coyote is king. He is neither startled nor afraid at the sight of a 65 Mustang racing to escape the loneliness of this landscape.

I take the wheel at Eureka where nothing is open. I feel certain we have enough fuel to make the last stretch to Fallon. It is a certainty that will crumble on the endless highway.

Wiz has been driving Sally hard through the night and soon collapses in the passenger seat. I have slept uneasily, on edge, but I am driven to overcome this strange sensation of danger. For the first time in our journey I feel threatened. The source of danger is the uncertainty itself. I am not familiar with the rules of this road.

Go into the darkness, the wise one says, and be not afraid. Destiny awaits. But I *am* afraid. I experience rabbit suicide from the wheel and it shakes me. It is beyond my control. I begin to settle, accept, and the endless highway calms me.

Wiz is still asleep when the sight of a stalled four-wheel drive vehicle greets me on the other side of the road. The driver is outside the vehicle and tries to wave me down. He is well dressed and his vehicle is fairly new. There is someone else inside the vehicle. All this I process yet I do not stop. I slow down and awaken Wiz, explaining the situation.

He says, "I'd sure like it if someone stopped for us."

I should turn around and go back.

"How is he dressed?"

"He looks okay."

I should turn around and go back.

"They should get some rest. There's nothing we could do anyway."

I am relieved. My fear is that if we stop we will not be able to go again. We're miles and miles from anywhere. We have driven Sally harder and farther than she has gone in a decade.

"We'll call the highway patrol when we get to the next town."

"They won't be stranded long."

Wiz goes back to sleep. I feel better when a semi goes by in the opposite direction. Semis have CB radios. All will be well. Still, it is strange and discomforting to be in the survival mode and to feel endangered by the simple prospect of stopping to help a fallen and fellow traveler. The mirror is unkind.

The sun rises in the east behind us, casting its mystical glow on the desert. The desolate landscape becomes clear with stark treeless mountains rising from the flatlands before us.

I have come to realize during the course of the night that I am less than certain about our fuel status. The gas gauge doesn't function. The tank had held twenty gallons before it rusted in the sweltering climate of Tennessee. The capacity of the replacement tank is uncertain.

Wiz wakes up a couple hours into the day and announces with a look at the road atlas that we are in a danger zone. I have no idea what that means or what the implications are and I don't care to find out.

There are postings in the sagebrush alongside the road, placed at approximately two hundred yard intervals about a hundred yards in. We cannot read them from the road.

My conclusion is: This is not a good place to run out of gas. I can't help but wonder if this is my karma for not stopping to help the stranded travelers.

The road before Fallon is far longer than its mileage. We enter the desert mountains. I coast on the downhill and whisper silent encouragement to Sally. At each crest I look for signs of civilization like the Donner party or the sailors on a lost ship.

We see murders of crow in random clusters, groups of five to seven. It is a comforting sign. The crow is still with us. At last Fallon appears like an oasis on the horizon. I pull into a gas station on fumes and count my blessings. We had survived desolation row, the longest and loneliest stretch of road in the land.

The gas meter reads 13.1 gallons. The attendant informs us that the danger zone refers to the local naval air station's use of the land for target practice. It seems it could have been much worse. The danger was more imaginary than real.

Still, I would not pass this way again.

7

FLIGHT OF THE GREY EAGLE

We are little more than a stone's throw from the High Sierras of California. In the beginning this journey was a trip to the Golden State.
"Going home," I said. "Wouldn't mind some company but I'm going just the same."
From the moment Wiz agreed to join me on the road it became much more than that.
The night before departure we recorded the jazz poetry play inspired by our meeting. We gathered our cast in an old school house in the hills of the Tennessee countryside. It took over five hours to record D'Arc Underground, a futuristic Joan of Arc, in an ordeal that tested our patience and will. Wiz controlled all sound, including keyboard, saxophone, trumpet and French horn – everything except the voices of the actors and the blast of cicada in the outside forest.
We embarked on this journey as jazz poets with a Nashville ally who gave references in Albuquerque and the San Francisco Bay Area. By the time we left New Mexico neither jazz nor poetry was at the forefront of our consciousness. We had become Zen golfers in the moonlight of Grand Canyon. We had become the spirit of the crow. We had witnessed the solemn march of death and played our part in it. We had leaped into the

darkness. We had heard the laughter of the Zen master. We knew fear and loneliness and witnessed beauty beyond belief.

Now we gather our thoughts and collect our visions for we will soon be called on to become social beings. My family is gathered just over the hill. I had not seen any of them for over a year. My aunt and uncle, my cousin and his wife, along with a scattering of mountain friends and acquaintances I had not seen in at least two years. My older brother, the forgotten one in the family (heroin formed a stronger bond than blood) had only recently returned from Arizona. I had not seen him in over five years.

The town of Graeagle is a family place. As kids we had often spent parts of our summers in this small sparsely populated mountain retreat. The people who made a living here were a rare and sturdy breed. It was a logging town back then. The men took jobs with the logging camps and lumber mills during the summer and scraped by the best they could during the winter.

Wiz could have made it a home. It was well suited to a man for all seasons, a jack-of-all-trades, and a man who could work with his hands. My Uncle Tim is also such a man, soft spoken and strong. The same could be said for his son, Tim Jr., who had overcome a reputation for his wild and reckless ways to become a man that could be counted on. His wife Cathy, of equally sturdy timber, had a heart of gold. She had a lot to do with her husband's transformation.

In the old days Graeagle was a paradise for hunters and fishermen. Over the years things had changed. Only an hour from Reno, Nevada – a fact that should have foretold its fate – it became the home of three championship golf courses and a burgeoning community of summer homes for the wealthy.

My aunt Zella, an angel with a curious skin condition whose onset coincided with the town's sudden affluence, had the foresight to start a gourmet coffee, candy, card and gift shop on Graeagle's main street. The shop thrived. She worked it herself for many years, watched it grow and moved it to a larger building down the road before finally turning it over to her son and his wife.

My mother, Artis, as sweet a human being as ever graced this planet, had taken to spending most of her time with her sister. It was a development I did not understand at the time. It left my father, a former professional boxer and policeman, feeling more alone than ever.

Artis and Zella found their own paradise on the Klamath River near the coast in northern California where my aunt and uncle owned a cabin. It seemed the gray eagle had flown north, leaving behind the old wooden Indian outside Zella's original gift and coffee shop. They followed their bliss.

The Fourth of July gathering in Graeagle had become a family tradition. My oldest brother John and his family started it many years ago. I joined in the last few years before my departure for Nashville. My sister Sue and her husband Robert were now a part of it, as were most of my siblings and their families.

Only one member of the immediate family would not be there. He stands out by his absence. I recall how often he spoke of this place with a sense of belonging. I know that he and his wife had separated for a time but they were now back together and she had given birth to their second child. I wondered what unresolved conflicts remained between them. The decision not to come to Graeagle was dramatic. The family welcomes me as they would a long lost son and takes Wiz into their embrace. There is always room for one more in the family of working people. Like Wiz, my Uncle Tim is Polish and is thrilled to share his heritage with the new arrival.

Wiz has an easy style and manner about him and connects with people of all ages. I envy that quality though I recognize it comes with a price: an obligation and responsibility to be generous with one's time. It is a blessing and a sacrifice but it is one he shoulders with grace.

We exchange stories and make plans. Tonight we celebrate; tomorrow we watch the parade, play a round on the local nine-holer and settle in for the fireworks display.

My aunt inquires about my wife, Sara, and wonders when she will get to meet her. I realize she may be wondering if she will ever get to meet her. Sara has instructed me to reply that we needed some time apart. I say only that she had business back in Nashville.

When I left she been recording in two studios: One as the artist and the other as a songwriter/musician. I am not aware that business has slowed to a crawl in the city of music. I have called only once and left a message on a phone machine. I am two thousand miles away. It has been a difficult year, a year of survival, and I want to be free of the debris it has left with me. I want to focus on the moment.

As I approach my fortieth birthday I am a married man. I am a speech pathologist in the public schools. I am a writer by avocation only. But tonight and for the length of the journey I am none of these things. I am only a man in search of his calling.

We spend most of the night in the motel room of my sister Sue and her husband Robert. Within the family Sue is closest to me in age and philosophy. Her husband has served as both counselor and antagonist in late night discussions on the meaning of life, marriage and everything else.

My sister once came to me on an obligatory mission to bear testimony to the power of the mind. She had taken a course on the techniques of mind control and affirmation. To her surprise I was receptive. She did not have to convince me. I believe in the power of the mind. She thanked me for affirming her own sanity against the storms of criticism and belittlement she received from other quarters, friends and family alike.

Over the years we would share our thoughts concerning everything from auras, meditation and altered states of consciousness to chakras, the power of crystals, karma, reincarnation and the afterlife, religion and the new age. Nothing reached beyond the realm of possibility and nothing would be trivialized, scoffed at or belittled. Our bond became closer than kinship. We regard each other with mutual respect, unconditional trust, love, and a shared sense of wonder in the world of ideas.

In some ways our bond served to protect her from the cynicism of our upbringing in an atheist family. After all, I had attained an advanced degree. The family respected my achievements and my intellect. I had always enjoyed studying, reading and writing. These qualities made me a more successful student than my brothers and sisters. It had less to do with my intelligence than my preference for academic pursuit but I recognized my position in the family hierarchy.

Each member of our family had something to distinguish him or her from the pack. John was a leader, an organizer and an enforcer of family values. Randy was a smooth operator, a dandy, a wild one with a social gift. Sue was the communicator, the spiritual one and the arbiter of disputes. Dave was a hard worker, determined and the best golfer. Bob was level headed and by far the best artist. Robin was the pretty one, the most sensitive and the best with children. Tom was the most imaginative and a genius with gadgetry and mechanics. We all had something.

Our family album is like a high school yearbook. Our trophy case is full.

We are joined in Graeagle by my long lost brother, Randy, who has been to the lower depths of drugs, poverty and self-imposed banishment. He has survived and returned to the family circle. Wiz admires his response to the constant preaching he is obliged to receive. Everyone means well. Randy listens quietly as he is reminded of the many times he has betrayed the family trust. He nods and replies, "I agree with you one hundred percent." He seems to mean it and has learned the futility of trying to explain the past. He is a recovering junkie. He speaks of friends – known to us all – who did not survive.

He recounts the story of an old family friend. Sue offers testimony of his kindness. Like Randy he was a good man who got lost in the shadows of an alternate lifestyle. He lived in a separate reality. Randy argues that he was not a junkie. His poisons were alcohol and cocaine. The drugs did not kill him as much as a broken heart. He had devoted his life to the woman he loved. When she left he fell apart. They found him laying on the floor of his apartment, drowned in his own vomit. With a straight face he tells me that if his life story is ever written it should be called: Sleeping with the Ants. I don't ask for an explanation.

Later, as we reflect, Wiz speaks of his own brother, who lived a wild life and died young. He remembers him as a good, even great man who lost his way. It is a ghost we share: the knowledge that within ourselves there lives a certain attraction to the dark side. There is cynicism. There is doubt. There is the blues. There is a wild rebel who, if not for the grace of God, would lead us to the abyss and bid us jump. His brother jumped. But he lives now as a constant reminder and haunting presence in the hearts and minds of those he left behind. He is remembered well for the good times and the love but there will always be sadness.

My brother is still alive. His spirit seems full of joy and laughter, his manner calm and easy. He has gazed into the eyes of the beast and lives to relate its meaning. At this moment, frozen like still waters in a moonlit pond, he has no need to return. I believe him because he believes in himself. We do not know what the future holds. We never know. But for now, in this refuge beneath the pines, he has come back to the family of light.

We spend hours trying to play a song they have written called *A Family Tradition*. Robert spends as much time explaining that he can't sing as he does singing. The late entrance of my oldest brother John finally interrupts us. He has succeeded my father as the one who now holds the family together. He has learned to temper his wildness with the wisdom his wife Margie has nurtured in him.

It seems a cop stopped them on the way here. He had been drinking and left his headlights on high beam. The cop let him go with a warning on the condition that Margie would drive the rest of the way. It serves as a warning to us all. Caution be the wind. We are all inclined to engage in reckless behavior in the spirit of jubilation. Caution. Behold the signs. We retire for the evening.

The next day we gather in front of Tim and Cathy's shop The Mill Works to watch the annual parade. Reminiscent of Norman Rockwell, small towns and a more innocent time in American history, there is a man, a Vietnam veteran paralyzed from the waist down, who has traveled the length and breadth of the country on his wheelchair to stand up for the rights of the handicapped. It is amazing what people can do with conviction and dedication.

The volunteer fire department, the logging industry, jazz musicians and jubilee dancers, the Sierra Club and developers are all represented. It is a slice of Americana that seems as distant at the seventh star of the Pleiades on a clear night.

Cousin Tim serves as a judge on the parade dignitary platform. The same man who once uprooted a kitchen counter and walked through a plate glass door in a nightmare vision of Armageddon is now a pillar of the community, respected by all.

The time arrives for a round of family golf. We have two foursomes. My father, who has been uncharacteristically in the background, takes charge. This is his element. Though he picked up the game relatively late in life, he passed it on to his children, teaching us the basics and instilling a love of the game.

He challenges our concept of Zen golf but when I ask him if he has ever guided the ball with his mind, something clicks. I have seen him summon the power of the masters in many a round but the spirit of competition stands in his way. He loves the game and he speaks often about its mental aspects. Nevertheless, he cannot leave behind his competitive nature and competition is the polar opposite of Zen. He is a master of gamesmanship. He loves to win and he desires the power of a younger player. In my view that is what blocks him from the mastery he desires.

It seems there is some confusion regarding our starting time that results in a two-hour delay. By the time we are called to the tee mental fatigue has entered our spirits. The group scheduled to go off in front of us is somehow intimidated. They ask us to play through. We decline but my father yells out: Don't let them fool you! They can hit the ball a mile!

We play through at their insistence. Pop's group is up first. He rips a low draw down the middle of the fairway. My older brother steps up and hits one wide left and out of bounds. My brother-in-law follows with another OB left. My sister adds two more.

One of the group that let us play through says: Well, I didn't know they were going to hit two apiece!

It doesn't stop. My group hits two more out of bounds. My shot is a dribbler but at least it stays in play.

I have seen this phenomenon before. Add a little extra pressure off the first tee and see what happens. If the player ahead of you goes astray you're more than likely to follow. One must learn how to clear the mind and begin again.

After a stumbling start, we settle down to golf. Despite an opening double bogey I finish three over par. My round includes a five iron to within six inches of the hole for birdie. Visions of the canyon are alive and well.

Our foursome has its ups and downs. My youngest brother fixates a bit too much on power. He struggles through eight holes but unleashes a 280-yard drive on the ninth. It is the talk of the day. His girlfriend, an attractive nurse with a pleasant disposition, is basically a beginner but she plays with finesse and poise. Little brother is a good teacher. His manners on the course are impeccable. Wiz surrounds a good number of pars and bogeys with a couple disasters. All and all, we enjoy the round, the walk and the company.

The atmosphere in the other group strikes a contrast. Only my brother-in-law, who also thrives on the challenge of competition, speaks of their experience. My older brother had taunted him about playing for money at a stroke a hole. Their scores are nothing to brag about but they are only a few strokes apart. Neither my father nor my sister has played particularly well.

Later I talk to pop about the unwanted effects of playing for power. He agrees and makes a promise to himself to make amends: Swing easy, hit hard.

My older brother crowns me the new family champion. The reigning champion, however, has not played. I sense family troubles creeping up, age-old sibling rivalries, and I want no part of it. Competition has played a major part in my upbringing and I have grown to recognize its value in instilling drive and inspiring progress but I have also recognized its darker side. The drive for mastery should come from within. The desire to improve and achieve excellence should be independent of one's competitive standing.

Should a player be less satisfied with his round if his playing partner scores one less? Hardly. There is nothing on the golf course more disturbing than one golfer reveling in the misfortunes of another. It happens all too often. It will inevitably express itself in his or her own misfortune somewhere down the line.

In the game of golf one cannot escape the laws of karma.

8

DOWN HOME IN THE VALLEY

Going home, going home, I'm a going home…

That sentimental melody from the film *The Snake Pit* runs a continuous reprise in my mind as we leave behind the clean, clear air of the High Sierras and descend to the valley where I was raised. In a country rich with indelible beauty from the glistening sanctity of the northwest coast, the barren solemnity of a sculpted desert, the tropical density of a southeastern forest to the surreal color transformations of a New England fall, this agricultural flatland is and always will be home.

It is not the first time I have lived away from the great central valley of California. As a young man I pursued the dream of an artist for the better part of two years in New York City. I returned home to complete my education and become a more useful or at least employable member of society.

Three vehicles leave Graeagle at approximately the same time on a Sunday afternoon. Wiz and I are in Sally, Robert and Sue are in their new four-wheel drive Cherokee and my father and Randy are in a rough-running 1985 Mustang – not a good year. The drive to Modesto is about 200 miles, normally a three and a half hour trip. After a half hour delay on interstate 80, Rob and Sue arrive in four hours. Both Mustangs, wary of a prolonged traffic jam and possible overheating, take the southern route. It will take pop nine hours. It will take us ten.

We choose the path of the journey or rather we take the road given. Instead of fighting traffic, we go with the flow and it takes us to a golf course in Truckee.

Two gentlemen who bear our own first names join us on the first tee. It is the first time I have witnessed Wiz introduce himself by his given first name. They are about the age of retirement, one a doctor and the other a lawyer.

The doctor seems an ethereal, easy-going man whose first choice of hobbies is tennis. His knees have faltered so he's chosen golf as a replacement. The lawyer seems more stoic and serious about the game. He has recently take lessons and is determined to put what he has learned into action. The doctor enjoys kidding his friend in a good-natured way.

We enjoy their company. They mirror us in ways beyond their first names. I wonder if they are a projection of the people and players we might become twenty-five years down the road.

They speak of the harshest winter in recorded California history. It came on the wake of an eight-year drought. They were snowed in well into the spring when finally the roads became passable. I am reminded of the Donner party and the storm that led to starvation and cannibalism. The doctor tells us it happened no more than a mile away as the crow flies.

The golf itself is unremarkable except for an incident that seems to send us all into a tailspin. On the fifth tee my ball sails left. Trees obstruct my vision but

I'm told it skipped by an older woman on an adjacent fairway. Wiz observes the event but is not yet sufficiently in tune with golf etiquette to yell Fore! in my behalf. I walk over to apologize but the lady is ready to explode with rage. I try to explain but it does no good.

I can't help wondering if I should have been more aware of my fellow golfers. One is never alone on the course. Should I have sensed her presence? Should I have been more conscious? Our playing partners advise me to shrug it off but we all begin struggling. At the end of nine we play three more just to recover our games. We wish our namesakes farewell, receive their best wishes and once again hit the road.

Traffic is still jammed as we head toward the western shore of Lake Tahoe. Twilight glistens on enchanted waters as we stop at a roadside diner for a meal and a bottle of beer. Wiz buys and I'm increasingly aware of his generous nature. We have noted that a section of highway 50 is closed. The waitress tells us that cars were sinking in a bad mixture of recently applied asphalt. We later learn that my father's car was caught in that mixture. Their journey takes them on a series of detours and almost comes to blows.

The jam on the interstate, caused by a fruit check, turns out to be the least troublesome. Nevertheless, our road is a series of jams, stop and go to the valley floor. We don't mind. Life is often a lesson in patience.

Wiz serenades a car full of young ladies on trumpet. They are thrilled as we chase them down the mountain in the spirit of the moment. It develops into a game of tease and tantalize. We pull off for coffee in Placerville and they move on with smiles and waves. It is the stuff of fantasy. It fuels the fires. Had they stopped we might have had an interesting conversation. Wiz might have continued the serenade but nothing more would have followed.

We arrive in Modesto, the city of my grounding, well after midnight. It takes some time to rouse my sister from bed. We exchange stories briefly and retire for the night. I have a strange sensation, a vague feeling as if I never really left.

9

MOTOWN

To the world outside this valley Motown refers to the Motor City and conjures images of Cadillac Records, Stevie Wonder, the Supremes, Aretha Franklin, Ike and Tina Turner. Here it refers to the city of Modesto, an appropriate name that translates from the Spanish to modest. I wonder how it strikes Wiz with its expansive flatlands, its Quik Stops and 7-11's, its Burger Kings and lighted ball parks, its almond orchards and shopping malls, its construction projects and its main drag, its blatant commercialism and downtown improvement, its tree-lined streets and industrial parks.

In parts of the Midwest I'm told it is known as Sin City. It is a major crossroad for illicit drugs. In my own travels I have never encountered anyone who has heard of Modesto except those who have been here. For years a controversy played out on the editorial page of the local paper concerning the absence of freeway signs directing drivers to Modesto. The population has bulged to over 200,000 residents.

To me Modesto is a lot like every town. It has changed with rapid growth and runaway development over the years yet it remains very much the same. Its young people still have trouble finding things to do outside the realm of sports. Its adults still complain about the rebelliousness of youth, the high crime and unemployment rates and the development of prime agricultural land.

Local politicians win elections on no-growth platforms but the developers always win in the end. The march of progress is unstoppable. It is a town of odd bedfellows and curious contradictions. The city council has outlawed the cruise, the tradition made famous by Modesto's own George Lucas in the movie *American Graffiti* yet they still re-enact the cruise one night each summer.

The one positive development I have observed is the downtown café where young people gather with books and notepads, listen to music and talk about art. It is an alternative to the bar scene. They look at their elders as we looked at ours with a measure of distrust. They seem to be gathering notes for their own cultural revolution. I like the look of them and wish them success.

A good friend of mine has contributed to the trend, opening a bistro called Deva after his oldest daughter. It tops the list of my places to visit.

Charlie is quite possibly the nicest guy in America. In over a decade the harshest criticism I've ever heard the man utter is: You must be high! I met Charlie through the crossroads of women and sports. At the time I was a student at the local college and became romantically involved with a woman from my old neighborhood. As it happened, her sister was married to one of the few remaining longhairs in town. That's how I met Ron, a gifted athlete, teacher and maybe the second nicest guy in America.

At some point Ron invited me to play softball with

the Westside Hammers. Charlie, another of the few remaining longhairs in the tradition of the late sixties, played third base for that team. Ron played centerfield and I manned left. Before long we began gathering at Charlie's place on Paradise Road, talking baseball, passing the pipe and listening to rock and roll. Charlie's main man is Neil Young.

My oldest brother John offered me a spot in the fantasy baseball league he had pioneered with his friends. I invited Charlie and Ron to join me as partners. As it turned out, that sealed the bond of our friendship. My participation in softball would end when I took a part in a summer Shakespeare production but the fantasy baseball would endure for decades.

Neither Ron's marriage nor my relationship would long survive but they enabled an enduring friendship. That's how life is or so it seems. As a playwright once said: Our ends never know our means. On the winding road of life there is ultimately so much to be grateful for and so little to regret. I love this life. I love the living of it. I love bending with the breeze and shaping my own destiny.

Above all, I love the people who have become a part of my life just as I have become a part of theirs – as if by chance. Charlie's wife Cathy is also a gifted teacher who has worked with my mother as teacher to aide. She believes in the spiritual nature of existence. She believes she has encountered extraterrestrial life on earth and she greets that knowledge with both wonder and apprehension. Ron's second wife, Deborah, is a wise woman from the sixties tradition. They both have children who from all appearances are gifted and talented, free spirits seeking to find their own ways to make a mark in this world of uncertainty. I like watching them grow up, their minds expanding to meet the inevitable challenges of life.

As we make our way to Charlie's café, the one word that describes both him and the circle of friends surrounding him occurs to me: Acceptance. It is a simple creed governing the conduct of this sacred circle that paradoxically requires a great deal of intellect to comprehend. There is no wrong where there is no harm. At Charlie's you are not judged by your opinions, your taste, your manner of speech, your appearance or the color of your skin. Everyone is welcome and valued for his or her contribution to the harmony of variance. Like Wiz, it is a quality that calls upon Charlie to give much of his time and energy. It is not his habit to cut a conversation short or turn down a friend in need. As a consequence he will often let his phone ring indefinitely without answering. Even nice guys need time to themselves.

I have never been to Deva before and my knowledge of its location is limited to a street without a crossroad or number. I know only that it's somewhere on Jay Street, a street that runs from the Westside to the center of town and feeds into the new main drag at five corners which in turn runs north by northeast.

My search begins on the Westside. In my mind I picture an informal atmosphere, low key and low overhead: A converted storefront with wooden spools for high-powered wires as tables, director's chairs placed here and there without pattern, a bar rather than a service counter, a sound system next to the cash register with assorted tapes and disks. On the walls I see avant-garde artwork, photographs and old rock posters in the psychedelic style of the sixties. Neil

Young and Crazy Horse is prominent, his Ragged Glory gracing the air. Wednesday night happenings, Thursday night jazz and Friday night rock, books of interest in a corner of the room and a water pipe just visible behind a potted plant.

In the back of my mind I hear Charlie saying: You've got to be high!

At length we find the place downtown, a few blocks short of the main drag. Times have changed. I realize that my vision was my own dream. Charlie is more the pragmatist. The bistro might have been subtitled: A Touch of Class or Fine Wine & Roses. The impression is upscale rather than subterranean. On the walls are large prints of the works of Van Gogh, Manet, Monet, Gauguin, etcetera, against a tasteful, wallpaper background. Classical music blends with the ambience. They have conceded Charlie one Neil Young ballad. The rest is classical. The décor is complimentary to a menu featuring Pesto a la Panache. Times have changed.

It is without doubt one of the finest café-restaurants in old Motown, marked for the uptown crowd of lawyers, judges and businessmen.

A beautiful and talented young actress who was the source of numerous unfulfilled wet dreams in the days of my youth greets us. She is our waitress. I offer that she has the ideal boss.

"You mean Charlie?" she replies with a smile.

I nod and realize this place has more than Charlie's imprint. I later learn he has followed the advice of a friend and restaurateur from Seattle.

It is the only establishment in northern California with Guinness Stout on tap – served at the recommended room temperature of a typical Irish pub.

That is Charlie's touch. He assures us his influence will become more prominent as time goes by.

Charlie finally makes his entrance and his eyes light up. We go through the introductions and Wiz is welcomed into the circle. Cathy joins us with a warm embrace. She speaks of a friend who has died recently in a solo car wreck at 120 miles per hour. By divine coincidence or random chance, I sent a message over the computer lines at the approximate time of his death. It read: *Is anybody out there?*

It went on: *He was a man who befriended many; who left his mark on the trees and park benches...and in the hearts of those he loved. He wandered long and far from home and returned to find no one who remembered his name. His mark erased, painted over by guerilla graffiti artists... Is anybody out there? Does anybody know my name?*

They were not words meant in effigy or as an epitaph. They were elicited not by the journey behind but by the journey ahead. Yet how strangely poignant they are at this moment. Death is a journey. It is the greatest journey of all and one that escapes none of us. As Charlie says: No one gets out alive.

He does not mourn. He will not mourn my passing. He remarks that this was the way he would have liked to go: Wild, reckless and free, like James Dean in a blaze of glory. I did not know him but in relation to Charlie, a man with a smile who offered words of encouragement. Did he mean to check out? No one will ever really know.

Ron joins us accompanied by his youngest child, Manon – named after the film *Manon of the Spring*. She is a beautiful child, full of life and laughter.

We all sit for a few on the house. The more things change, the more they remain the same. Baseball,

David Lynch, Neil Young, the times. We are invited to dinner and a gathering of minds. Of course we accept and make our way to Sally with Manon coaxing Wiz into a little music on the streets of Motown.

The journey brings out the child in us all.

We crown her a Princess and she crowns us King and Jester. With some difficulty we depart. The gods of golf are calling once again.

10

GOLF AT THE OLD MUNI

Modesto has three public golf courses. The oldest is a nine-hole course next to the river and the minor league ballpark. We call it Old Muni. It is the equivalent of no name at all since all public courses are referred to as municipal. Just the same, it is a distinctive course that holds a lot of affection in the hearts of those who learned to play the game here.

It is a flat course but its layout offers a good test of skill. Tall trees – maple, sycamore, oak and pine – line the fairways. Some holes bend to the left, others to the right, challenging the golfer to shape the shot.

The finishing holes offer a fair sampling of all the shots in golf. The seventh is 475 yards, par five. For a long hitter it is easily reachable in two except for a line of trees that cut off the right side of the fairway at a little over three hundred yards off the tee. It requires a draw, bending to the left and clearing the tree line. The second shot then presents a choice. You may be able to reach with a fairway wood but you must avoid a large sand trap guarding the left side of the green. Lose the ball to the right and you're out of bounds, two-shot penalty, end of tournament. The safer option is to lay up with a five iron to the right side of the fairway, taking the trap out of play and leaving a short iron to an open green. A third option is to drill a two iron to the front of the green, leaving a chip for eagle. It carries the same risk as a fairway wood to a lesser degree. Unless you're as hot as a pistol and in that zone where you can do no wrong, the safe play is the best play.

The eighth hole is a standard 150-yard par three to a large sloping green with a wide and deep bunker on the left. Pin placement is key. If the hole is short right you can fire an eight iron at the stick. If the hole is up left the bunker comes into play. Take aim at the pin and you risk the trap or worse, skipping over the backside for a delicate chip back. The best play is an easy seven to the middle of the green. Take your chances with the putter.

The ninth is a classic and one of the toughest holes in the valley. A long par four, sharp dogleg right, with a road bordering the entire right side and a tough bunker guarding the left of the green. A power fade off the tee leaves you a long iron or fairway wood home. There are few things easier in golf than losing a long iron or fairway wood to the right. The shot calls for a low draw. If you hit the trap you want to enter it from the green side, leaving a relatively easy sand shot.

I love old Muni. We used to play those final three holes over and over until the sun fell and you could no longer see the flight of the ball. My only eagle (two under par on a single hole) to date came on the fifth hole, a short par four. I chipped in after a solid drive.

Muni has the added feature of a free driving range with just enough room for a good five iron. I went to high school just down the road. We'd spend five dollars a month for unlimited play. Ironically, I was not in love with the game back then. It was the late sixties to early seventies and I had plenty to occupy my mind. I began hitchhiking in those days and had plans to join the flower children of Haight-Ashbury in San Francisco or Telegraph Avenue in Berkeley. I nearly dropped out of high school in those days.

It was a time of change and upheaval that left no one unmoved. I had my first taste of mind opening drugs. I went public with my views on religion and watched the alienating effect it had on so many of my peers. It was a time of great promise in the universe of ideas and I wanted nothing more than to be a part of it.

There was so much I did not understand in those days. As high school graduation speaker I accused the president of lying to his children as he escalated the war in Vietnam. More than anything else I represented the frustration and sense of betrayal that my generation felt. In the wake of Kent State and Jackson State we became targets. In the wake of the crackdown in Berkeley, the Watts riots and the brutal suppression of dissent in Chicago, we were disenfranchised.

And the worst was yet to come.

For me as for countless others, the assassination of Bobby Kennedy was the ultimate betrayal. I had seen him only days before on the back of a campaign train through the central California valley. All the joy and promise I once felt soon turned to a pervasive cynicism. I felt betrayed not only by the powers that be but by the elders of my own generation. To have offered so much hope and then, just as I prepared to join the march, to fade so easily into the back pages of history.

It seemed a cruel fate to be born at precisely the wrong time: Old enough to be aware but too young to engage. It would be years before I understood well enough to forgive them and forgive myself. They were lost. They had nowhere to go. There was nothing they could do. There was no greater plan and those we had empowered with our trust were suddenly gone, dead and gone. We thought we could change the world by faith alone. We were wrong. Jim Morrison became the spokesperson of the alienated generation and James Dean became our hero. Dead and gone.

Survival was the first rule of the revolutionary and the one we overlooked. Too late. Much too late.

We who survived would carry on in our own individual ways. It would be years before I could recover enough faith to enjoy the simple pleasures of life, love and games like baseball, where the great drama of life is reenacted in microcosmic detail over the course of spring, summer and fall, and golf, a game that more than any other sport or pastime is a pursuit of individual faith.

It is Saturday morning and we arrive at old Muni just before tee-off. My father and our other playing partner are on the putting green. Mike is my longest standing friend in Motown. We share common interests in baseball, theater and golf. We met during our college days when we were members of a national championship speech team. He made his mark with a rhetorical analysis of Lindberg's anti-war stance in the forties: the tainting of an American hero.

My greatest glory was a gold prize at the state championships for my portrayal of Woody Guthrie in Readers Theater. That show went professional in 1973, playing the college circuit for a year and sending my ambitions soaring. Within a year I had written, directed and acted in my first play: *Fosdick & Muldoon*. I moved to New York and returned to the valley two years later, humbled and shaken.

Mike was a member of the cast for both the Guthrie

show and my play. I had typed him as an accountant whose central motive was to win at any cost. There is a lot of history between us and a lot of memories.

Our compadre in those days was a man who married Mike's sister only to divorce after a continuing struggle with alcoholism. He was one of the most intelligent and levelheaded individuals I have ever known. There but for the grace of god…

At one point he called upon his friends and family to provide support in his battle. I felt acute discomfort sitting in a circle listening to the testimonials of harm, pain and despair that each in turn provided. My days with him were full of joy and laughter, glory and adventure. He had been no source of harm to me. He had failed as a friend only once and then at the urging of our professor in competitive speech. He abandoned our debate partnership – not the crime of the century, just a disappointment.

But I was told these harsh accusations were critical to his recovery. I sensed that I was too far removed from his current life to be of help. In truth I might have felt the danger of trying to save a drowning man.

The last I heard from him he was doing well. A dedicated member of Alcoholics Anonymous, he had begun a new relationship. From the depths of my heart I wished him well and offered what I did not then know was a major truism of AA: One day at a time. Don't look back, brother. You can never look back.

I wonder now if what drove us in those college days was not some basic insecurity. Maybe we sought external recognition to compensate for some deficiency in our upbringing. Our ends never know our means.

Mike is now an accountant for Stanislaus County. He is married to a woman his friends half-jokingly call a saint, a title she does not claim. She has without doubt helped him, along with a somewhat successful EST experience to overcome his temper.

Wiz recognizes a few glimpses of that side of him in his game. It is not a welcome trait anywhere but particularly not on the golf course. In the past, it has been Mike's habit to curse a wayward shot and talk incessantly about his own game to the last person on earth who wants to hear it: his fellow golfer.

But Mike is in control today. His game suffers from his obstinacy and a lack of attention. He does not seem interested in improving his game. He is only interested in improving his score. He does not understand the relationship. I have learned not to offer advice. I have come to believe that a person's game need only be good enough to enable him or her to enjoy the walk.

My father is in his element. Old Muni is his home course. He smacks one down the middle, long, lean and mean. Wiz finds the trees left, Mike skies one far right and I chunk one about a hundred yards. Pop remarks it is one of the worst shots he has seen me hit. His memory is not as good as it once was. I make an excuse of the road but I know there are no excuses in this game.

Back to the basics: Balance. Without balance there is nothing. I recover and hit the green in three but three-putt for a double bogey. I make note that I should warm up before the next round.

Pop, whose nickname from his boxing days is Killer, has a number of tactics for unnerving the mental state of his opponents. He doesn't go so far as to chatter while a fellow golfer putts and he holds his comments while a player is preparing to strike the ball to a whisper but they are nevertheless designed to unsettle his opponents and they often work. Because of these tactics I have had difficulty playing with my father. But he is my father so I have learned to accept them as a challenge to my ability to focus and concentrate on the shot. While I still gesture for silence when others address the ball, I have enjoyed the rounds we have shared since that time. On the golf course we have achieved a level of camaraderie and mutual respect we rarely experienced when living in the same house.

Pop is a great golfer and in many ways a great man. He has fought for the things he believes are right. He has inspired in me a respect for truth and justice.

When he stays within himself and honors the limits of age, he is the kind of golfer who compliments you on a good drive (well past his) and then steals your breath (and the wind from your competitive sails) with a 30-yard chip to the center of the cup for par. As with life, one of the great challenges is accepting your limits.

I double bogey the second hole in the same manner as the first: bad drive, good recovery and three putts. I save par with a good wedge shot on three, take a tough bogey after a booming drive on four and par out the nine. The last three holes I play by the book. On seven I take the tree line out of play with a drive bending left, play a mid iron to the right side and a wedge to within eight feet of the pin. I just miss the putt. On eight, with the hole up left, I play to the center of the green and two-putt for my par. On nine I follow a power fade with a low iron to the front of the green and finish the round with a chip and putt.

A strong finish draws me even with pop, who has played well despite a few careless shots. It has been a good round. We have all played well enough to enjoy the walk and Wiz has thoroughly enjoyed my father's company. We gather in the clubhouse for a beer and a conversation that touches on golf, politics, Nashville and Modesto. Others join in. Everyone at old Muni knows pop.

When we were growing up, my father was a policeman and a wrestling promoter, a local celebrity. Most of his life he had a place in the spotlight. Even as a kid he was a star athlete. As a young man he became a top ranked prizefighter at a time when boxers were respected like baseball and basketball players are respected today.

His kids (all eight of us) were pretty much awed by his collection of trophies, photographs, press clippings and tales of the ring. His prized possessions include a championship belt representing all of allied China, Burma and India during World War II. He had a sterling silver trophy in the shape of a boxer from the same tournament, proclaiming him the "most scientific boxer." Pop loved that trophy. Finally, there was a black satin jacket with the Golden Gloves emblem on it. He once said that I was his only son who might have had the skills to succeed in the ring. He gave me that jacket.

Acting as his own lawyer he sued his former boxing manager for skimming the purse (a common practice in the pugilistic profession) and won. He used that settlement to start up his own gym in Motown. For some time he trained boxers and promoted boxing but there proved to be too much risk and not enough profit in the boxing game. Quality boxers demanded a large purse up front. If the event didn't draw the promoter took the hit. He went into professional wrestling and rock promotion. Wrestlers, while controlled by a regional manager, worked on a percentage basis, and rock concerts had a lot of appeal in a town that offered so little to young people.

I have vivid memories of the day two young Hispanic fighters pop had trained, one of whom became a star of the local ring, decided they could challenge the old man. Pop took them on back to back and knocked them both out within two minutes. The young boxers suffered a blow to their confidence but my father secured his larger-than-life stature in the eyes of his kids.

He was the man who brought Jim Morrison and The Doors to Modesto only weeks before Light My Fire hit the airwaves.

His promotion of rock concerts eventually led to the end of his career as a police officer. After nearly twenty years of service as the only cop trusted on the Westside during the days of racial unrest, the new chief did not appreciate rock and roll. My father didn't appreciate the new chief or many of his policies: ticket quotas, duck ponds (places where cops sit in hiding, waiting for a hapless car to violate the vehicle code), preferential law enforcement and the phasing out of older cops.

Pop fought his dismissal and won a contested personnel hearing against all odds but the local powers that be conspired to ignore the findings and dismissed him anyway. A corrupt lawyer, who had been a state representative and volunteered to represent pop, failed to file the appeal until past the expiration date.

I was there when he advised pop to sue him. Pop couldn't figure it out. He couldn't accept the betrayal of a man he considered a friend. The lawyer was in on the fix. He knew pop didn't have the money to continue the fight in court.

I don't know why he did it or what they had on him but I knew at once he threw the case. The city had spared no expense defending itself in a non-binding personnel hearing. They hired a sitting circuit court judge who subsequently moved up to the appellate court bench. He did everything he could to skirt the civil rights issue around which the case evolved.

My father's lawyer advised him to save the issue for an appeal that would never be filed. He instructed pop not to take his case to the people. That was when I became suspicious. Pop was winning in the court of public appeals. But my father took his advice. He believed in him. The man came from our side of town. He was an important man and pop wanted to believe in him. It took him years to come to the same conclusion I drew back then: The man was a rat.

The local newspaper played its own part in this small-town conspiracy. They had assigned the story to an enthusiastic reporter who possessed a clear sense of what was happening. The paper pulled him and the story fell from front-page news to back-page filler.

I remember my father's dedicated search for a critical piece of evidence documenting the chief's corruption. There was a news article I recall reading in which the chief and his lieutenants advocated an ordinance requiring businesses to purchase alarm systems. What the article did not state was that those same individuals had started their own security alarm business. They stood to gain a lot of money.

Pop spent hours in the county library trying in vain to hunt down that article. It vanished – as if it never actually existed. The mayor, who had advocated the need for a citizen's review board, was called to testify and turned to mush. The case was too large for the mayor's office.

I learned a lot from this experience. I learned that I could not count on cops or politicians to be honest and to do the right thing. This was the way city hall fights back against anyone who stands up to the machine.

It crushed my father's spirit. He was only months away from full retirement but they could not allow him to retain his job after such a challenge.

Pop ended up selling his wrestling business and began working as a security guard here and there before taking jobs in the bay area, Reno and finally Portland, Oregon. There he suffered a heart attack on the golf course. He returned home to have bypass surgery. I was at his side when he awakened to this world after surgery and held my hand for dear life.

It was a strange sensation to be holding the hand of this proud man who had thrown off his religious upbringing and stood alone as an atheist of conviction. I could feel his fear of death.

I remembered a play called *I Never Sang for My Father* and wanted to be sure he knew my love. Everyone in the family was changed by that experience – a little wiser, a little stronger. Life goes on.

Of all the words the great Dylan Thomas ever wrote the only ones I've read and disagreed with are those that began and ended, "Do not go gentle into that goodnight; rage, rage against the dying of the light."

I believe that this life is but prelude to the great mystery ahead. We should not race to its end but neither should we fail to accept and even embrace it. But the poet spoke for my father at this moment and I could only empathize.

Within three years, my father's father, a wise and deeply spiritual man, my father's sister, who had fallen into the snake pit and returned, his mother, who was always kind to her grandchildren but who deeply distrusted all men, and his brother, who had been a joyful man but in the end betrayed my father by handing the family inheritance to an opportunist, would all be dead. Like my father, maybe they expected too much in life and, with the exception of my grandfather, too little in death.

Pop is the last surviving member of his core family and in many ways he is more alone than ever. In a very real sense he is the tragedy of the American family.

My mother grew apart from him during his wandering days. She grew stronger, partly out of necessity and partly through the influence of the women's movement. After more than two decades as a mother, housekeeper and manager of the family business, she re-entered the workforce. In her forties she learned to drive for the first time. She learned that she possessed a gift with children and got a job as an instructional aide. Over time she secured her own modest retirement and began to spend more and more of her time in Graeagle and Somes Bar by the Klamath River with her sister Zella.

The family is proud of her strength and fortitude but saddened that it came at the price of my father's pride. She broke free from her dependence and they would never be truly close again.

Now it seems my father lives mainly for golf, for the camaraderie and competition it offers, and the hope that my mother will forgive him and return to his side. He cannot live in the secluded surroundings of Somes Bar or the mountains in Graeagle. He needs the familiarity of the valley, the company of friends and family, as much as he wants her affection.

Let go. Let go of the things you love and the things you love will find you. Let go of your feelings of guilt and betrayal to rediscover your own self-worth. Sit still in the winter of your discontent and behold the beauty of life. The best is yet to come.

We say so long to pop and start off on a second nine. A local known as Golfer Joe or sometimes Joe the Pro, a curious character who has known more hard times than an Appalachian tenant farmer, joins us. He appears to be in his early to mid forties and dedicated to making the senior pro tour on his fiftieth birthday.

Outside of our group, he is the only familiar face left at old Muni. Everyone else seems to have been alienated by rising fees and the changing attitude of the new staff. They have moved on to other courses. Once golfers are alienated, it is hard to win them back.

Joe tells us he's been able to pick up a few bucks teaching golf lessons but he's worried about the job situation. The off-season unemployment rate in this valley has reached about forty percent. He talks about coming to Nashville or seeking his fortune on the mini tours in Florida and Carolina.

I tell Joe that times are rough all over. I am not aware of Nashville's unemployment rate but I am very much aware of its homeless problem. People in Nashville are amazed when I tell them I found a job without much trouble.

It is difficult to concentrate on your game when you're listening to someone's story. Joe has an up and down round while showing off his new titanium shaft, oversized driver. He hits them long but not always straight. I play well, pick up a birdie on five and finish the nine three over par.

On number eight I go for the stick and end up ten

feet short. Wiz sends a seven iron stiff to the pin. It hits hard and skips to the back fringe about fifteen feet from home. We leave the stick in as he lines it up, addresses the ball and strokes it dead center. It is his first birdie. The memory and the satisfaction of that dead solid stroke will last a lifetime. It is a blessing to bear witness.

Wiz buys the beers at the clubhouse. All and all, it has been a hell of a round of golf.

That's what I love about this game. You can skull it, scrape it, chunk it, slice it, duck hook, shank and yank it for seventeen holes and then...magic. The game teaches you to hang in there. Never give up on a shot. Never give up on a hole. Never give up on a round. Why? Because, if you still believe that anything can happen, then anything can happen. Anything you can imagine in a round of golf is possible. I am still waiting for the magic of a hole in one. Twice on the very hole that Wiz birdied I have been as close as you can get. One hit the stick and settled inches from the cup. The other marked in front of the hole and finished directly behind it. One day it will go in.

Wiz's birdie goes a long way toward keeping the faith. Hang in there, buddy, it will happen.

11

SHADOW OF DEATH

    I'm not certain how it came upon us. I could only piece it together afterwards and still I am not clear.
    The day began with taking care of car business. Sally was overdue for an oil change and some loving care. We then played the front nine at Dryden on the Tuolumne River, just down from old Muni. I played well with a birdie on five (a short par three) and a regulation par on six, the toughest hole on the course. It is a long par four dogleg left. It would be hard enough without a huge oak in the middle of the fairway about two hundred yards down. I hit a solid drive to the left of the oak and stiff a five iron to the back of the green. I finish the nine two over par.
    I can't quite remember how Wiz played except that our playing partner, a hotshot who is eager to give us tips, compliments him as the most relaxed golfer he has ever seen. It's true. Wiz is a master at freeing his body of tension and swinging with a natural flowing motion.
    We have the famed Dryden cheeseburgers and kill some time driving around the old hometown. We read jazz poetry at Mancini Bowl in Graceada Park in the heart of town. It offers an interesting sidelight that I share with Wiz: In this conservative city still stuck at the tolerance level of the fifties, it is said this park, the

central park of the town, is named for a lesbian couple. I speculate that in Modesto, as in many places we have encountered across the country, the feminist solution to the AIDS epidemic is lesbianism. However misguided, if the fundamentalist right is right about AIDS being the wrath of an angry God, then God must embrace lesbians.

As I near the end of the first chorus of D'Arc Underground, a drunken Hispanic man in ragged clothes rises from a park bench and grumbles his displeasure. He tosses the word Satan at us. He gains my attention and raises my ire. As I've said, the piece from which I read is the story of Joan of Arc. The charge of Satanism should not surprise me but it does. It startles and disturbs my peace of mind. Determined not to be censored in my own hometown, I finish the chorus and flip to the demands of the underground:

We demand food for hunger free of charge!
We demand jobs for all who call and ones that suit their make and model not their shoes!
We demand the laser stun be drop and done or access free to all!
We demand the opening of the boundaries, free travel, an end to border stops and crossing!
We demand the closing of the righteous guard!
Let them work to feed the poor!
We demand access to the stars!
Let all behold the heavens and scope the upper maze!
We demand a home for all and not a hole to shovel dirt in!

I finish and we depart to the unexplained silence of our drunken critic. It hits his button. He says nothing but he knows he is wrong to judge. Maybe next time he'll think again. We are his advocates yet he would gladly have slit our throats if he had the chance.

We make it over to Charlie's place on Paradise Road for an early dinner. The road called Paradise is where high school kids ran drag races in the bee-bop early sixties with Wolfman Jack growling on the AM radio and crew cuts glistening with Dixie Peach. It was also where one of my first loves lived. We were eighth graders at Mark Twain Junior High on the Westside. She was a cheerleader and I was vice president of the student body government. She was six inches taller and thin as a rail. In my eyes she was as beautiful as any Hollywood star.

We danced all night in the age of innocence. That first slow dance to the crooning of Johnny Mathis is a feeling that will never leave my soul. The end of that wonderfully sweet and tender romance, a split born of miscommunication at the beginning of our high school careers, was my initiation to the world of relationships. It is an experience I would not trade for any other.

In contrast to the cuisine of his downtown bistro, Charlie is basically a meat and potatoes guy. His dinners are down home affairs. There's usually a parade of visitors. They are all good people and they are welcome.

Wiz entertains the kids with improvisational flute and piano. The youngest are truly inspired. There will be music in their lives.

We move outside where Charlie plugs in a tape of D'Arc Underground. I suggest turning it off after the first chorus but he insists on playing it in its entirety. It runs nearly two hours and draws encouraging and insightful comments. Charlie says he's heard a lot of stuff that's way out there but at least we're out there with a purpose.

It is the first time anyone beside our selves has heard the recording from start to finish and their encouragement means more than they know. It has been a long winding road in the jazz poetry world and I'm in need of a little affirmation. We are reluctant to leave this treasured company but the obligations of time press on.

We return to Robert and Sue's house where we find they are being entertained by one of Robert's old friends. He is a fine musician with the mind of a businessman and the ambition of Caesar. He's fallen on tough times. The band he has been promoting in the bay area, featuring a great old Chicago blues man, has broken apart, his marriage has failed and he has recently been diagnosed with kidney failure. Wiz joins him with his magic flute but his guitar goes silent when Wiz plays and he engages in distracting conversation.

I become aware that Wiz is struggling, despondent and weak. I am only vaguely aware of the cause but a sense of discomfort settles in my soul. We are due to visit my closest friends down the road in Turlock. Patty and Jere teach theater at the university. They are rehearsing a production of Chekhov's *Uncle Vanya* and that has prevented me from seeing them until now.

I suggest it is time to depart and Wiz is more than ready. In the car he tells me he cannot breathe. A dark presence has taken hold of him and won't let go. I let him catch his breath before telling him what he could not know. That old friend of Robert's, a friend that turned on him in trying times, is a dying man. It is the shadow of death that shrouded him and follows us even now. Making matters worse, a growing sense of discomfort and vulnerability takes hold of me. I feel like there's a hole in my aura. My vision is discolored, warped and twisted. Something needs to happen. Something must relieve us of this cloud that hovers over us like a pall at a funeral dirge. Wiz begins to chant in the tongue of another world. It seems to have a calming effect, like an ocean sunset. I join in the chant but the ghost will not leave.

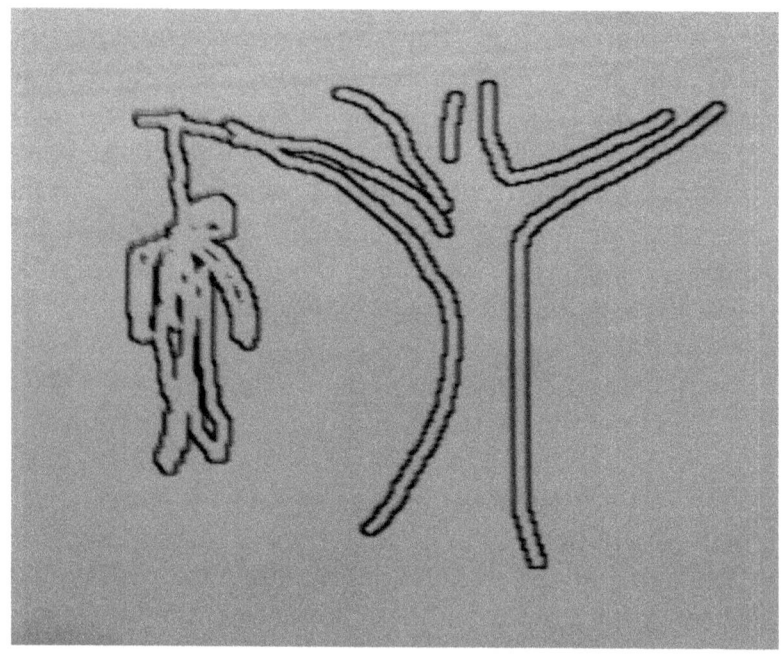

It strikes like a bolt of lightning in a summer storm
Invades the solar plexus like a veiled omen
Spreading like a cancer like a hellish nightmare
On a sleepless night

As we near our exit in Turlock, Sally checks and sputters. Something is desperately wrong. We glide to a stop. We're out of gas. After traveling 2,500 miles, traversing high mountains and desert plains, land of every description from Nevada's desolation to the peaks of Donner Summit, here by a familiar Turlock exit we run out of gas. Something has happened to break the spell. It could have been worse. It is a strange blessing and inspires caution. We have been running hard – maybe too hard.

Wolves howl at a clouded blue moon
Owls take flight
The air stills to an unnatural silence

Wiz stays with Sally while I walk a short distance to a gas station. It is time for reflection. Too much recklessness. Too much late night partying. Too much blowing with the wind. Too much trust where trust does not belong. Too little grounding. Too little self-control. A man must learn to play the safe shot where the safe shot is called for. Going for the pin each and every time will surely lead you astray.

We struggle in to the company of friends, the shadow subsiding but still clinging to us, the weight of it bearing down hard. At last we arrive and instantly sense that we have entered a sanctuary. The shadow is gone. We could not outrun it but we could evict it by entering a sacred circle of unconditional trust.

Purity of heart and soul guardian angels above
Circle of unconditional love
Diffuse the darkness dry the fear
Smooth the furrowed woe
Blessed friendship sacred light
Like the first beacon on a jagged shoreline
Like the first breath of spring

Wiz later refers to them as saints. On this night, at a moment of need, they are indeed guardian spirits, like the canyon crow.

If a person is lucky enough to be born into a warm and caring family it is a blessing of chance or fate beyond our comprehension. The people we find thereafter with whom we find it possible to share our lives with mutual respect and understanding is a blessing of choice. It is something we value and search for much of our lives. When we find it we should not abuse it by holding on too firmly or leaning too heavily. We must learn to be a blessing to those who bless us.

When I moved to Nashville only a year ago, it was as difficult to leave this circle of friends as it was to leave my blood family. "Let go, brother," said the drowning man, wise beyond his experience.

Liberated from the shadow of death Wiz plays with abandon, soaring to untapped heights, tapping unknown depths and soothing our shaken souls. Patty is enthralled.

A superb actor and director, she has become a politician of sorts by accepting an appointment to chair the local arts council. After years devoted to raising her son Jack – an incredibly talented, quick witted and sensitive eight-year-old – she has established herself as a major force on the local theater scene. Her eyes glow with enthusiasm and purpose.

Her spouse Jere, who has become the first tenured acting instructor at the university, tells us about playing the kind of part in Uncle Vanya he always avoided: a romantic idealist. He has thrived in the role of a villain. The first time I saw him he played an engaging Salieri, Mozart's evil nemesis in Peter

Shaffer's *Amadeus*. He now embraces his softer side and it will without doubt serve him well.

My old friend Gary, a talented actor whom I had worked with on a number of projects for the stage, also joins us. He has a calm about him that is rare. He has no job at the moment, having quit his last job due to a back condition that doesn't allow him to stand for long periods. He is working with Patty and Jere now and is being paid for his part in Vanya.

Gary should be an acting instructor. He has the talent, the experience and the wisdom to be an excellent teacher but he is haunted by a mistake from the past. While working as an elementary teacher he was busted for selling hashish. It was many years ago at a time when it shocked the general populace but not nearly as much as it would today. Had it been expunged from his record his life would be very different than it is but in the small-town mentality of this valley records are never expunged. Still he is well and he offers us an I Ching reading as well as a quote that came to him while waking one morning:

"At last the wanderer understood: it was the cup, not the water. It was the journey, not the spring. It was the search, not the drinking."

A feeling of peace, contentment, and a mood of calm reflection and joy surrounds them and carries over to us. It is only days before opening night. Typically there is a lot of tension.

It grows late and we reluctantly move on. We will see them again and thank them for an inspired performance. We make a golf date with Jere and Patty though it will keep us here longer than intended.

It remains difficult to let go.

BAY AREA POETRY SCENE

We have had little time to reflect since we arrived in Modesto – in fact, since we left Nashville. The commitments of family and friends have left us with a desire to continue the adventure of the road.

We have one day open and we decide to sojourn with the reputed king of the bay area poetry scene: Jack Foley. Wiz knows him through a mutual friend and fellow poet from Alabama. Jake Berry is a poet's poet, a master craftsman of words, an inventor of language and an architect of letters and imagery. His name in the underground circle of poets is legendary. Poet, musician, songwriter and graphic artist, his seminal work *Brambu Drezi* as well as *Species of Abandoned Light* have found a noted publisher in San Francisco.

Wiz is convinced San Francisco will embrace our cutting edge style and revolutionary content. I am less certain.

We start out early and ascend from the valley of agriculture past the windmills of Altamont Pass, where the spirit of the late sixties died with the Rolling Stones concert that gave birth to the film *Gimme Shelter*, and veer north to the city of my youthful dreams: Berkeley, California. I have witnessed great changes in this city since the days when I used to thumb a ride, hang out in university square listening to the drum line, roam Telegraph Avenue in search of a new nation, study the hip in cafes and crash by the wooded creek that ran through the campus.

I remember a beautiful woman in beads, layered dress and painted face who smiled and kissed my cheek as if to acknowledge the promise of a better world. Wet dreams of youth.

I remember the mystical force that ran through this chosen place like an electrical current of pure hope. I remember the radical speeches, political pamphlets and sitar blended with Jimi Hendrix electric lady land. I remember the spirit of love and the sense of infallibility juxtaposed with hardnosed cops wearing blue helmets and carrying black riot sticks. I remember the time they stormed People's Park and the time they cleared the courtyard in front of the library with canisters of teargas.

The entire history of the sixties movement, from birth to burial, is recorded on the walls, in the streets and in the spirit of this city.

Everything has changed.

We walk down Telegraph toward the university. Street people, once the heart of a cultural revolution, are now a homeless problem. Tie-dye and jewelry venders are too stylish to be hip. We hear little music and no discussions of politics. The electric lady land is gone. There are only memories.

We walk to the square and the library steps where Mario Salvo addressed throngs of student activists during the Free Speech Movement – a movement crushed by the American right's future wonder kind: Ronald Reagan. The students now seem serious and politically correct but their issues are microcosmic: tuition, affordable housing, parking and smoking in public places. No one wants to change the world; they just want a better back yard.

There are musicians here. We find a lone bongo player and a guitarist but Wiz senses they don't want accompaniment. They have staked claim to their own turf. Music for money's sake.

We move on and stake our own claim. Wiz pulls out his magic flute and lets loose a kaleidoscope of sound that lingers in the air before drifting with the wind. I wait for the wave and jump on.

A karmic debt is mounting like invaders at the shore
Another land to conquer
Another face to scorn
With every tick of the cosmic clock
Another soldier off to war

A karmic debt is spreading like an incurable disease
Plunder every mountain
Poison every stream
As each tick of the cosmic clock
Brings death in a gentle breeze

A karmic debt is building like a river overrun
Pledge allegiance to the Profit
Turn around and walk away
With every tick of the cosmic clock
Another promise is undone

Following Wiz's lead, I move from politics to wet dreams to underground jazz and back again. We gather no crowd of followers but those in our midst take note and gesture approval. A man with the eyes of a writer sits to our side, observes closely, trying it seems to read our minds.

Satisfied that we have made a mark we walk back down Telegraph, stop at a familiar café for a bite, pick up a copy of *Zen and the Art of Golf* at Cody's, a renowned local bookstore, and say goodbye to this city. The transition from the core and center of political activism and thought to a progressive university metropolis is difficult for those of us who remember. But these are still good people, worthy successors in their own way. Something had to follow the revolution and this is it. It may be that the people who populated the streets of protest are still here but they've adapted to the times.

The revolutionary's first law is survival.

Wiz leads us to Jack Foley's house in the plush hills of Oakland. He greets us as if we are long lost brothers, speaking with the kind of enthusiasm usually reserved for the young. He drops names like an actor on the make: Sam Shepard, Kerouac, Burroughs, Ginsberg and Michael McClure. He is involved in a weekly radio show that features himself, McClure and Ray Manzarek of The Doors. He offers us samples of his recordings and hands us scores of poetry magazines. His theory is that the root nature of poetry lies in the oral tradition of Homer, the first poet of the western world.

I find his exuberance engaging and fascinating, like a child showing off his toys the day after Christmas. He has the appearance of a poet in his fifties with his frazzled hair, loose clothes and sandals. His wife strikes a contrast, straight and proper, but clearly devoted to her husband and his artistic lifestyle.

Despite their beautiful home they worry about

money. They worry about their teenage son who has no interest in poets or poetry. It is all too typical: the offspring of rebels seek identity in opposition. Conformity is the new rebellion.

We continue our conversation at a charming little Chinese restaurant where Foley engages an unknown couple in a discussion concerning the origins of the term Pot Stickers. The man has something to say about virtually everything.

I put the meal on my credit card. Having made his comments about money concerns, he seems pleased and maybe surprised. Jazz poets from Nashville aren't known to carry a lot of cash.

In parting, he recommends a club in San Francisco to try out our poetry and Wiz slips him a CD of D'Arc Underground. We share hugs in the brotherhood of music and words and drive away.

As we cross the Bay Bridge on our way to The City, I realize that we have spent over four hours in the company of a whirlwind mind. Ironically, it approximates the length of a round of golf. It is a rare pleasure to listen to a man so eager to share his extraordinary life. A part of me wonders if his passion for theory and topics of little apparent interest is misplaced but it is overcome by the acknowledgement that passion of any kind is a rare and valued commodity.

It is not chosen but chooses. It is his calling and mine is not to question it.

We reach the poetry venue to discover that nothing is happening. The readings are over. A bearded man, who might have been a professor or a computer genius, plays chess with a young intellectual type. I sneak a peak at the small stage in the back, a bleacher before a naked podium with room enough for about twenty spectators. It occurs to me that poetry is a very small universe. I begin to doubt that there is any future in it – not here or in Nashville, not in Albuquerque or Chicago. Those who engage in poetry have large dreams but small ambitions. Those who devote themselves to the poet's life have very large hearts. They are not driven by success – which is too often measured in humility – but by the essence of the thing itself: The Zen of poetry. If poetry is an oral tradition it is enough to stand before an audience of five and let the words be heard. Let them roar like a stampede of buffalo or quiver like a lover's lips in a moment of soft ecstasy.

Wiz and I have dreams and ambitions to match. We do not yet understand the Zen of poetry. We depend too much on the response of our audience. We want to please and be pleased.

Wiz is a musician. Music is his first calling. He has been known to play for hours from some secluded perch in a forest. I am a writer. That is my calling. Though I may never be published and my plays never performed on a professional stage, I continue to write. I will always write. Just as the music itself, in a perfect moment, is enough to spur Wiz on in an endless quest for something sacred, the act of committing words to paper is enough for me. Even if those words are read only by a few or not at all, I will continue to write.

Every writer wants his words to live on just as every composer and musician wants her music to reach generations beyond our own. But that desire is not the reason an individual creates. A writer writes, a sculptor sculpts, a painter paints, an actor acts and a musician plays because it speaks to the center of his being, because it is a passion that cannot be denied. As it is with art so it is with golf. As it is with golf so it is with life and everything in life of value.

We walk out of the poetry establishment and perform our piece on the street corner. A few glance at us in passing but no one listens. We drive down Van Ness into the heart of the city but nothing pulls us in. We decide to drive south toward Santa Cruz and Monterey.

It is late when we reach Santa Cruz so I suggest we stay over and ride the roller coaster in the morning. Wiz wants nothing to do with it. He surprises me from time to time. He is not usually a man to step back from the promise of adventure, even a cheap thrill like the famous boardwalk roller coaster.

We are both in a curious, reflective mood. We drive on, still waiting for a sign or something that attracts our attention and calls to our spirits. Nothing does.

We finally lay out our sleeping bags at a small beach with a Polish name. The saltwater scent of the Pacific, the sound of the waves and the ocean wildlife has a calming effect. We awake just after sunrise to the hustle of farm workers on their way to the fields. We shake off the reflections of the last twenty-four hours, pack our bags and drive into Monterey where one of golf's most transcendent experiences awaits.

Dollar per hole, Pacific Grove on Monterey Bay may be the most beautiful golf layout in the world. The opening nine consists of tree-lined fairways while the back nine is oceanside links style, open to the elements. It features a handful of cypress, tall wispy grass (the gorse) and ice plant on banks of sand dividing fairways. If you've ever had the experience of trying to hit a golf ball out of ice plant you know how difficult it is. It may look easy but if you try using anything longer than a wedge, good luck. The fairways are narrow, the rough punishing and the greens are generally small but undulating. The course places an absolute premium on accuracy.

When golfers refer to this place as the poor man's Pebble Beach, they are talking mostly about the back nine. The story goes that a resident who loved golf and wanted the game to be available to all donated the land to the city. He made his donation contingent on two conditions:

First, that it be used as a golf course. Second, that it should always be affordable to people of modest means.

The story is often told whenever I come to this course and today is no exception. We arrive early and are paired with a twosome of retired gentlemen, reminding us of our namesakes in Truckee.

We play well enough on the front nine and settle in for some inspired golf on the back. There are a dozen deer wandering the course along with scores of seagull, crow, squirrels and jackrabbits. It is a spectacle of nature that rivals Grand Canyon. It is a place to forget your game and allow yourself to soar with the wind.

The sight of number eleven, looking out over the Pacific, a family of deer grazing below an elevated tee, brings out the best I have: A solid three wood, a stiff wedge and a ten-foot putt for birdie. On twelve, the most breathtaking hole of the round, a par five bordering the coast, with cypress revealing the shape of the wind, Wiz lets loose a booming drive and a fairway wood that challenges imagination, expanding the limits of his game. Here in the grandeur of the California coastline, the game itself takes on new dimensions.

We play well, score well – though the latter no longer matters – and hit the road with a newfound sense of wonder.

Moving on to Carmel – that charming coastal enclave for the rich and famous, where Clint is King or at least mayor and the shops are tourist friendly – we enjoy a natural high and a feeling of infallibility. It seems nothing can stop us and then a pigeon nosedives into the grill under Sally's hood. The timing is beyond belief. It leaves me dazed. I am unable to process this phenomenon, a continuation of Nevada's suicide rabbits, to a satisfactory conclusion.

Maybe we are in need of grounding. Maybe we are too high and too centered on ourselves. The pigeons have long been attracted to Sally's Mustang orange exterior, pelting her with droppings at every opportunity. Maybe this is Sally's revenge.

I believe in life. I believe in the sanctity of life and would not take life from any being except in the most dire of circumstance. I know only that I do not know. I understand that I do not understand. Like the mesmerizing power of the sea, like life itself, this strange episode of animal behavior is and shall remain a mystery.

In all the world I have seen nothing more beautiful than the cypress of Monterey. This is the home of John Steinbeck and a living tribute to the man's devotion to and indeed humanity's universal fascination with the sea. When I was a younger man it was my habit to come here when my mind was cluttered with trouble and despair. I would sit for hours, my feet buried in the sand, or above on an overhang where the seagulls would trace the shoreline. The gentle but all-powerful waves of the Pacific would empty my mind, cleanse my soul and send me back to the world reborn. I have the same feeling now. Wiz has supplied me with an old trumpet and a mute. We stand in the sand, him with his flute, me with my muted horn, and send sweet sounds into an endless sea. The crows are here and they seem to listen. Of all the times I have been to this beach over the years I can only recall gulls. The mystery deepens.

Wiz gives me a quick lesson on how to look cool while playing trumpet. We walk back to Sally and deposit our instruments.

We have come to this place in service to my memories. We have played a glorious round of golf in the kingdom of wildlife and natural beauty at Pacific Grove. Wiz has played shots neither he nor I thought he was capable of playing at this stage in his game. We have played with free and open minds absorbed in the majesty of our surroundings. We have had communion with the sea.

We have one more service to perform. We find our way through a maze of alleys to Hog's Breath Inn, Clint's place in Carmel, where I once saw the famed actor dash in and out, a beautiful blonde at his side, to check on his affairs.

Wiz asks the time and I realize we are due back in Modesto for a family picnic. A couple of attractive middle-aged ladies check us out with a notion or so it seems. We are immune. Clint's not in so we cut our visit short and hit the road back to Motown.

The drive back is peaceful, full of thought and dreams and pleasant memories. I realize it will likely be a long time before I will feel a Pacific breeze again. Letting go is hard.

We stop at a gas station in the little valley town of

Los Banos where Wiz calls ahead to let the family know we're on our way. He takes care of the gas and encounters a young lady, attractive but with a frazzled appearance. As we pull out he tells me her story. A man tells her it's his birthday and she offers him a present he'll remember. She looks Wiz in the eyes and says: Hell, I'd give it to almost anyone. She looks our way as she climbs the stairs to her motel room across the street. She charges the imagination. I tell Wiz he'd better wear two condoms for that action.

We drive away with the weight of the road a little heavier and the stuff of wet dreams [2] swirling in our minds.

[2] The original working title of this project: The Grand Canyon Zen Golf Wet Dreams Tour. I had written a series of "wet dream" jazz poems.

13

FAMILY GATHERING

It is an evening picnic in the large back yard of my brother John and his wife Margie's house. We had called from Los Banos but no one was inside to take the call. Everyone in the family is gathered outside, including those who could not make it to Graeagle.

My brother Dave is here with his wife Lisa and their two children. Cameron is a precocious seven-year-old who seems to be overcoming the only child syndrome. The other, Matt, is an infant whom I have seen only once. As I have noted, Dave is the family's best golfer. He is also the most cynical – a title I might have earned not so long ago. He is a technique golfer in the Jack Nicklaus tradition.

I once loaned Dave five hundred dollars at a time of need without making him suffer through a lecture on overspending. For that he is grateful. He won my admiration in return for his diligence in repaying me. He is the only person I have ever loaned money who did not require a reminder of the debt. I have become aware that loaning money is often the surest way to end a friendship but in this case it solidified our bond.

Dave is an honest and honorable man who, like my father, rejects all matters of faith. He is skeptical of spiritual concepts. He is skeptical of affirmation. He doubts the power of the mind, the concept of karma and the possibility of enlightenment. He believes in honor and hard work to the extent that it frustrates him when these qualities are not rewarded in this world as they should be.

He and his family have been through hard times but they have endured and now seem content. His wife Lisa seems to reflect his qualities: extremely intelligent, highly competitive, talented and hard working. She too has an edge of cynicism. It's interesting to watch them on the golf course. They demand more of themselves than they expect in others. It is little wonder he has pretty much given up the game. If he cannot live up to the level of play that once allowed him to break the course record at Dryden Park, why bother? They do not enjoy the walk.

Their demands on each other nearly cost them their marriage. But now all is well and I wonder if they have made some discovery. Perhaps they *are* beginning to enjoy the walk.

The next generation of the family now numbers six with one on the way. Bob's wife Robin has given birth to their second child and Margie is pregnant with their third child. Given that she had her tubes tied it comes as something of a surprise. There is some irony in the fact that my sister Sue, the most spiritual of the clan, wants a child desperately but has been unable to fulfill that desire.

Coming from a large family, there was a time when my parents began to wonder if the future of the family was secure. They need not worry any more. The children have become a dominant presence. They are the markers of time, the center of focus and the primary topic of discussion.

This gathering, however, is for the childless, wandering son from Tennessee. We talk about Nashville, my marriage, John Prine, the music business, the forest, ticks and chiggers and the sweltering summer heat. I realize that I alone have strayed from the nest, drawn by love and romance and a dream of stardom that now belongs to the woman I married. I alone have broken the chain. I lived for the better part of two years in New York City, pursuing my own dream of artistic fulfillment. Now I live in Nashville.

The time for wandering has pretty much passed in my family. Only the youngest, Robin and Tom, lack their own family ties to bind them to this locale. I sense they are unlikely to leave. Like a certain species of magpie, they are attached to the geography. They both possess a seed of rebellion that expresses itself it various ways: Driving too fast, partying too late, relationships that come and go with the wind. Robin attended school in Texas, Tom in Oklahoma, but they both returned home and show little inclination to wander again. There is comfort and security here. Though it can be stifling it is reassuring.

The age of the journey is coming to an end. One prominent symptom of the change is that there are so few hitchhikers and those there are seem wanderers of necessity rather than seekers of adventure. The next generation though rebellious in its own right, seems less interested in the journey as a path to spiritual growth. Maybe they've grown cynical in response to my generation's futility or maybe they have learned what Henry Miller learned late in his life at Big Sur:

Sit still and watch the world go by while all the things you need come to you.

Tom has asked about my philosophy that embraces

the journey within and the road to wisdom. I started him off with some of the books that inspired me: Hesse, Kerouac and Castaneda. They never took hold. They failed to reach out to him as they had to me. To each his own. In the end we must all find our own way. It is one the tenets of my journey: there is no single path.

Our days in Motown are numbered. There is a growing sense of urgency that I intentionally do not define. Time rushes at us. We spend what remains of the night and most of the next day at Robert and Sue's house, telling tales, kicking old dogs, exchanging thoughts and enjoying music. Robert is in rare form on the trumpet and with a microphone. My brother Randy joins us. He has formed a bond with Robert. They are like children reborn, singing and recording songs only slightly off key. I am convinced that Randy has a chance to rebuild his life [3]. Much of his transformation may be due to Robert's way of delving into the center of one's being.

I am surprised he does not probe into my life on the present journey. Maybe there is no need. He may already understand what I am only beginning to realize: I am no longer a part of his world. I may never return home and my visits may well grow further and further apart in the expanse of time.

I may be wrong in my assessment of the family roles. Randy has also been an explorer. He has been to the belly of the beast and wrestled with the dragons of his innermost self. That is a place I have not been and have no desire to visit. His experience leads me to question, to think and think again, to seek a greater understanding of the world. For that I thank him.

There is no single path.

Wiz and I must move on. We excuse ourselves and drive back down to Turlock for the long awaited production of *Uncle Vanya*. The performance is inspired, the finest production of Chekhov I have seen – though I admit I am not a fan. Patty plays the object of desire. She personifies the life force in an environment of decay. It is a familiar role and one she plays with natural grace. Jere is the enlightened physician who observes the relentless march of destruction in the deforestation of the land and seeks an antidote in the affection of another man's wife. He will not be denied by the moral code of a dying world.

Gary is death personified. He controls the great machine that ravages the land and sucks life from all who inhabit it. His character confronts the most tragic fate: growing old without comfort.

An old friend, who has been on a great journey of his own, plays the title role. Jack has married, relocated to Seattle, returned and is now preparing a move to Dublin, Ireland. I have watched his talent blossom under the tutelage of Jere and Patty. He plays the part of a humble man who has lived by the rules, worked diligently and suffered without complaint only to find his interests, his dreams and desires discarded in the rubble of a fallen world. Despite everything he loves life and confronts the tragedy that he will die knowing so little of it.

I am surprised that this play moves me. It speaks to our world on many levels. Are we decaying in our very souls? Have we lost our zeal for life? Are we destined to meet our ends with the realization that our lives have not mattered? *Life!* is the rallying cry. Live and have no regrets. That is the purpose of my journey. Enlightenment must follow life. It cannot escape or transcend it. Without life in all its dimensions there cannot be wisdom.

After the play we gather as we so often have at Jere and Patty's. Wiz finds harmony with Jere's brother John, a talented guitarist.

As the conversation moves on from the play my focus is drawn to Gary. He is at an age that I have come to believe is the age of the shaman – at least for my generation. He was twenty-five in the summer of love. He has observed a phenomenal transformation of the world through the eyes of an adult. He comes from an unhappy childhood and shares with Wiz a story of abuse at the hands of a nun in parochial school. Wiz has had a similar experience.

I wonder if these women, empowered by the cloth of faith, realize the mark of cynicism they have left on the world. It is a miracle that those abused children grew up to be the men that stand before me now. Maybe it served as their initiations. Maybe it helped them to break free of the ties that bound them to an obsolete creed. Their wounds have healed.

Gary preceded me on the path of wisdom blazed by Joseph Campbell. He is the sage that enabled us both to reclaim our faith. Once I believe in no religions; now I believe in all. I believe the essence of all religions is the same. I believe they represent a universal mythology and that this universality, far from reducing their value, empowers them to speak to all of us. I believe Gary understands this far better than I do. He has achieved a certain wisdom if not yet enlightenment. I give him copies of my latest works in the hope that he will understand my intentions and shed some needed light on them. I wish him well as we depart deep into the night.

<<>>

We have two more rounds of golf before we leave this valley. We will play the course in Manteca with Jere and Patty and Creekside, Modesto's newest course, with Robert and Sue.

Manteca is a beautiful valley municipal course. It features tight, well-kept fairways, a variety of terrain, water hazards, sand traps and a major wind factor on the back nine. Jere and Patty opt for an electric cart. Wiz and I will walk. We share some of our ideas regarding Zen golf – a topic that is not new to them. Patty is receptive as always and Jere is less skeptical than he once was. "It's not the shots; it's the ride," he proclaims.

Wiz makes some amazing shots and scores the second birdie of his golfing career, adding to the mystique of the Zen approach.

We take the turn in good shape but the back nine begins to wear on us. On the sixteenth hole the foursome behind us drills a couple of drives beyond us as we look for my ball in the woods. While we're on the green another shot skips past us to the right.

I linger on the next tee to issue a stern rebuke to their conduct. The force of my voice surprises both them and Wiz. Wiz later says he has witnessed the redneck side of my character but in my mind it is no less than what the game demands: respect your fellow players. You are not alone of the golf course. In the future I hope they will be more cognizant of those around and in front of them.

The incident affects my game. I double bogey the next hole and we all struggle in. It is a reminder: Our fellow players are as much a part of our games as the trees and the wind.

The damage is not so great. Our scores are respectable. This round has not been about the walk or the ride. It is about camaraderie. We have enjoyed the company of friends on a glorious day and we are both humbled and grateful.

Creekside was billed as Modesto's championship golf course. It is something less than that. It is far too short and its trees are a good ten years from becoming the barriers they should be. It is a good layout but nothing exceptional. Like Jere and Patty, Robert and Sue choose to ride while we prefer to walk. Having acclimated to the humidity of Tennessee, the dry heat of California goes easy on us.

It is a good day for golf and I'm on my game. Good golf like bad is contagious. Somewhere along the front side we all hit our strides and play well. An errant second shot on the ninth costs me a sub-forty round but it hardly matters. We grab a bite at the clubhouse and begin the back nine in good spirits. Like Manteca, the wind picks up as the day goes along and the back nine is wide open.

We allow a series of twosomes to play through. They are excellent golfers but I wonder if their speed of play is excessive. I speculate that they are gamblers who have chosen golf as the field upon which their bets are placed. Robert is a gambling man. I have seen him in high stakes action on the blackjack tables in Lake Tahoe. He is surrounded by an aura when he goes on a run. He speaks of it in mystical, even spiritual terms. The force that propels him feeds on the positive energy of those around him. Then it feeds on itself. It becomes its own entity and it is something to behold. It is the

Zen of gambling. There is no other way to describe it. Though the concept is foreign to my experience, golf enables me to understand it. I know the feeling. I've felt it. The energy of life becomes focused and channels into one cause. The effect is inevitable.

I cannot pass judgment on the chosen venue. It does not matter if it's golf, bowling, darts, basketball, pool, gambling or any path of artistic endeavor; it is all one. It gathers at the center of one's being and unites the one with the all. It is the essence of faith and the wonder of the human experience.

I am driving exceptionally well and on the thirteenth hole, a long par five with a tail wind, I let loose a monster. The ball rockets down the left side like a rifle shot. We will measure it at three hundred and ten yards [4].

As the others take their turns at the tee an elderly gentleman playing solo approaches. He is the image of Sam Snead with his easy manner and small straw hat. We invite him to play through and he graciously accepts. He steps up and hammers a drive with a smooth, even-tempered swing. As the great Julius Boros said: Swing easy, hit hard.

The old gentleman tips his hat and delays his departure just long enough to tell Wiz that the fairway wood he picked up at a yard sale is a classic persimmon and highly valued.

As we trail behind him, I notice that he walks to the longest ball as if by instinct. It is not his. He pauses and scans our foursome from a distance until his eyes meet mine. The old master is impressed. I give a satisfied nod that he returns as he retreats to his own ball. He hits his second to the front of the green and two putts for a birdie. By the time we reach the next tee he's long gone, like a ghost of golf's past.

It is for me a perfect moment, leaving me feeling exhilarated. I play inspired golf, birdie the fifteenth and finish the back nine in even par. On the sixteenth my sister finds her game and rips a series of excellent iron shots. She walks on air and her joy is palpable. Robert reaches the greenside bunker in two but takes three to get out. His temper flares and he hurls his wedge. He later claims he only tossed it aside as he retrieved his putter. Somehow the contrast between Robert and Sue strikes me as hilarious. I fight back the instinct to laugh.

To Robert's credit he recovers his balance and finishes a fine round of golf. We have all played well. It is a good and fitting farewell to the game in the great central valley of California. Tomorrow we're back on the road. Our first destiny is Wawona Golf Course in Yosemite National Park. It has been a wonderful visit and all I could have expected. Like a solid last shot in a round of golf, it will leave me with a desire to return.

[3] In the end it did not work out. Randy went back to his old ways. Old habits die hard.

[4] This was in the days of the wooden woods when a three hundred yard drive was exceptional.

14

YOSEMITE NATIONAL PARK

We have stayed three days longer than we intended. Once again I am reminded how difficult it is to escape the hold of this valley, this land and its sturdy, giving people. Modesto is like a variety of tree that grows here known as Trees of Heaven. Once it takes root it does not let go. It spreads and swallows the land.

Our plan begins with golf at a place called Wawona at the southwestern tip of the park. It is a place of infinite beauty that Jere and Patty have told us about. Our route takes us through Merced, a town smaller but strikingly similar to Modesto. In fact, all of these valley towns – Bakersfield, Fresno, Merced, Stockton, Modesto, Sacramento, Lodi – are only variations on the same theme. All seem to me victims of massive, unplanned urban development.

An army of Bay Area commuters has lately invaded the valley. It is a boon to real estate but a nightmare to renters and working people who are rapidly abandoning their dreams of home ownership. Thousands of people prefer to drive two hundred miles a day rather than pay the high price of housing on their home turf. Maybe they have no choice. The workers are being priced out of their own communities.

As we turn east into the Sierra foothills I remember

an ill-fated bike trip a friend and I took along this same path. We set out from Turlock with our sites set on Yosemite, carrying packs on our backs and a whole lot of grit. We took no precautions – no tools, no flashlight, not even a spare tire.

My friend had neglected to wear underwear and developed a rash. I recall his climbing slowly up these hills, his pack bobbing and swaying from side to side as he struggled to avoid contact with his bicycle seat.

We slept in a cow pasture in pitch-black darkness not more than a mile from the nearest town. We made it as far as Mariposa the next day when a burst of rain provided an excuse to turn back. A flat tire in Merced ended our adventure in humility. It was nevertheless a memorable journey.

My friend and I were as close as Wiz and I are now. We were brothers or so it seemed. But that friendship or at least its closeness would end several years later. I was directing a play and signed him up as my set designer. In fairness he was reluctant to take the job but I managed to persuade him. On one occasion he interrupted a rehearsal by moving set pieces around on stage. When I objected, he walked out.

Within a week we got the news that he had been in an accident. He rolled his car on the freeway. It seems he lost consciousness while driving. He had always been a risk taker and an adventurer. This time he had tested the limits and lost. He was fortunate to survive but he lost control of the muscles and nerves that moved his left eyelid. It is fixed in a closed position to this day.

He was an excellent actor and, in his own way, a prince of a man. His flair for comic acting was unrivaled in this part of the country. Like many gifted performers, his journey took him constantly to the edge. When he pushed too far he fell into an abyss. Some would say he jumped. The wonder is that he came back to carry on.

Would it have happened had I not confronted him for something that now seems so trivial? Would it have happened had he not walked out? No one can say what might have been. We would eventually become friends again but we would never be close.

It is as it is meant to be. I must remember this, learn from it, and hold on to it when it is my turn to take the fall. I don't believe things happen at random. One of the primary lessons of the journey is this: There is a reason and a purpose to the events and experiences that cross our paths. We should not fear or avoid them. However unpleasant they may be, we should embrace and learn from them.

We turn south at Mariposa and wind our way to Wawona. Throughout our journey we have repeatedly been advised to plan ahead and take precautions but we prefer to take our chances. If it is meant to happen it will; if it is not, it will not.

Does this make me a fatalist? I do believe in fate. I believe in magic. I believe in karma. I believe in spirits. I believe in the soul. I believe that every sentient being has a destiny. I believe there is infinitely more beyond our grasp than within it. Do we have a choice? Yes. We have a choice to either embrace it or deny it. Deny it and you deny yourself. Embrace it and grow. We must embrace our destinies in order to become the beings we are intended to be.

I first confronted the charge of fatalism in high school at the hands of a well-intentioned geography instructor. I had written what I considered an excellent essay on a subject that escapes my memory. I remember well the disappointment I felt when the paper came back branded with a red-letter B and the comment: Isn't this a bit fatalistic?

It was the first time my work was judged not by the quality of my writing but for its content. It would not be the last. It sent me into a tailspin of doubt. Years later I would explore my beliefs concerning destiny, fate and fatalism but at that young and impressionable age it only felt unjust. I deferred to authority and sought a more acceptable point of view but I do wonder if it delayed the journey of my soul.

At the entrance to Yosemite the ranger waives the fee with the curious statement: We're not charging today. We have now visited two of America's most popular national parks free of charge. It is how it should be and we accept the blessing.

Wawona is far from the glacial valley of Half Dome, Indian Caves, Yosemite Falls and El Capitan. It possesses a more placid beauty with tall redwood pines and open meadows of tall grass and wildflowers, nestled in a terrain where the gentle foothills begin their transformation to the High Sierra peaks.

Wawona Lodge is a large white wooden structure of southern grace, with a long row of elegant columns running the length of the lodge and bordering its front porch. Countless squirrels, ducks, swans and deer appear on its expanse of manicured lawn. They seem to blend with the boarders in soft white, blue and pink pastel attire. Everything is so graceful.

With plenty of daylight left we check in at the clubhouse. It doubles as the Wawona grocery store. We are invited to tee off any time we like.

We are at the top of our games through the first four

holes. We note strange warning signs at the first and third tees. The first tells the story of a seven-year-old child who lost his life to a deer. The second warns of a rattlesnake without rattles. In other words: Stay out of the rough.

The fifth hole takes our breath away. It is a long par four from an elevated tee, dropping at a steep angle to a small and bunkered green. Tall redwoods press in on both sides, giving the impression of a narrow tunnel. I try to control my tee shot, constricting my muscles and upsetting the natural rhythm of the swing. The ball sails right into the forest. I'm forced to take a drop, dribble my next two shots on a downhill lie and end up with a triple bogey.

Striking a contrast in a smooth, relaxed groove, Wiz plays the hole like a pro: Tee shot down the middle, second to the front of the green, chip and a putt for par.

As we make our way to the next tee, Wiz brings up our scores and jokes about the fall of the master. I'm not sure if he's aware of it but he has thrown down the gauntlet and raised the banner of competition.

Wiz has the tee and misfires into the tall grass. He declines a mulligan. I step to the tee and send a three iron sailing two hundred yards and slightly left of the mark. It gently fades and settles in the center of the green. The gods of golf are with me. I save par on the seventh with a great sand wedge and Wiz continues to struggle. He drops seven strokes in two holes.

He later claims it was only meaningless patter, an awkward expression of his trademark sense of humor. The gods disagree. He has not learned that even our expressions of humor have a dark side. They are far from meaningless. I have often seen one man's sense of humor turn a pleasant day into a constant battle. A misplaced joke, a comment that demeans despite its intention, has the power to end friendships.

Today the golf gods have delivered a stern lesson. Whether Wiz chooses to accept it is completely up to him. Golf is ultimately a game of humility. Wiz will have his day. As I have often told him, though I have acted as his mentor, he will better me as a matter of course. It will happen. But it is not likely to happen on a day when he is brash and over-confident. It is unlikely to happen when he raises the red flag of competition. It will not happen today.

We finish the round in good spirits and head for Yosemite Village as the sun sets slowly on the western skyline. Night has descended by the time we arrive. We are a little surprised to find the village store still open and a nightlife happening. As I wander off to find an open restroom, Wiz purchases a small flashlight, two pints of Sam Adams Boston lager, a fifth of cognac and a couple of microwave Mexican food platters. He starts up a conversation with a wide-eyed teenaged girl. The thought that runs through our minds is nothing short of absurd. We have been on the road too long.

We find an outdoor picnic table in front of the snack bar and watch the young ladies who seem to dominate this scene. Except for the tamales the Mexican platter is by far the worst excuse for a meal we have encountered. No matter. The beer is great.

We amble back toward the parking lot, scouting the surroundings for a place to sleep, when I spot a couple of park rangers. I wonder if it's cool to have an open beer on the park grounds and Wiz jokes: If they stop us we'll just have to kill them.

I stay with Sally while Wiz explores the terrain with

his little flashlight. He finds a place to lay our bags on the backside of the park headquarters so we pack up our things and head off. Again he jokes: If they catch us we'll just have to kill them. We settle in for the night to reflect on the journey behind us as well as the journey ahead. We have discussed crossing Tioga Pass during the night but fatigue and hunger hold us back. We accept the delay as part of the adventure. We have had a wondrous journey to this point. We are both pleased. Wiz observes that we could easily have come to hate each other by now. The road can be a difficult place for friendship and camaraderie but we both agree the journey has strengthened our bond. It is the first time we have looked back. Now we speak at length, retelling stories and recounting our own perspectives on the events of the last two weeks. We finish off our beers with a splash of cognac and yield to sweet dreams and visions of tomorrow.

    We awaken with dawn in a world of absolute grace, seeming frozen in time. We leave our empty bottles at the front of the building where they are sure to be spotted and discarded responsibly. Wiz does not want to risk being seen carrying them to the nearest garbage can. I make a vow to balance our karma by picking up trash down the line.

    Unable to find coffee, we content ourselves with cans of coke from a vending machine and set out for Tioga Pass. We are soon overtaken by the magnetic pull of Yosemite's natural splendor. We decide to hike to Yosemite Falls and I retell the story of the first time I got drunk. It was on a sixth grade field trip when a friend turned to me with a strange concoction of wine and alcohol by the name of Bali Hai. Beneath the majesty of Yosemite Falls I became as sick as I had ever been in my young life. It seems I have always had friends who were attracted to the wild side.

It is early and we are alone in the splendor of John Muir's valley. We linger long enough to collect our thoughts and become as one with the animal and indigenous spirits that still reign in this holy kingdom. Then we resume the journey.

15

TIOGA PASS

Tioga Pass is a long two-lane highway that cuts through the heart of Yosemite and climbs to an elevation of nearly 10,000 feet. The glare of the morning sun on the winding, twisting road makes the going rough, slow and treacherous. Not knowing why, I remark that if the pass were closed for any reason it would cost us hundreds of miles and a full day's travel.
 I am grateful we did not take on the pass last night. Soon the road opens up and the going is easy. We are about thirty miles from the village when a park ranger flags us down. He relates that a fellow ranger was shot during the night. The pass is closed until the suspect is caught. It might be within the hour or it might take days. We ask if there's a place we could rest to wait it out and he directs us to the lodge at Wolf Creek.
 We thank him but before we can turn Sally around he asks for a second time: Are you sure you don't have a gun in the car – not even a little one? Wiz has joked about carrying a gun and I give him a glance before answering: no. Not even a little one.
 We hear several versions of the shooting but the one that sticks is: the ranger came upon a man walking down the road and pulled over to ask if he needed help. The man said no but took off running into the

woods. The ranger followed and the man fired two shots from a .22 caliber pistol. That's a little gun. The ranger is alive and presumably will be able to identify the gunman.

I suddenly realize we are suspects and begin to think about some of our offhand comments taken so lightly at the time. First there was Wiz with his "we'll just have to kill them" and then me with my remark about the closing of the pass. Wiz is chasing thoughts in the same direction. He tells me that the empty booze bottles we left at the park headquarters could collaborate our story. I relate that if they decided to search Sally the first thing they'd find when they opened the trunk would be the word "Killer" on the strap of my golf bag. The bag had belonged to my father who still used his boxing tag. Nevertheless, it would be enough to keep us here a long time.

Then Wiz delivers the kicker: Unknown to me, he has stashed a gun in his bag. Shivers run up and down my spine. It does not sit well. I don't ask what caliber and don't want to know.

At Wolf Creek we are greeted by a gathering of stranded fellow travelers waiting for the restaurant to open. A line has formed and a woman emerges from the lodge to explain that her lodgers have priority. We politely step aside to allow the few lodgers to move to the front of the line. The hours drag on and the gathering of the stranded grows. They relate their own versions of the shooting and speculate on the identity of the suspect. He could be miles away in the desolate high country or he could have doubled back and got in his vehicle. He could be right here at Wolf Creek. He might be one of us.

Suddenly all single men begin to look suspicious.

Some fall out, making the decision to turn back and replan their vacations. We decide to wait. We indulge in a great breakfast and enjoy our interactions with the waiting staff. They are a joyful presence and yet another blessing on the journey.

We pull out our instruments and Wiz gives me a quick lesson on trumpet, teaching me a simple jazz scale. Before long the lesson gives way to jazz improvisation and space music. The sounds are sweet to my ears and seem to belong with the rustic surroundings. We are joined by fellow travelers and invite them to play but they are content to listen.

A dark-skinned man with a large pack and a noticeable limp draws all eyes as he walks into camp. He is an American Indian who is walking a trail that will take him from the Mexican border all the way to Canada. He has been slowed by a fire-walking experience that left a large blister on his right foot. Some park rangers arrested and detained him for carrying a weapon in the park. The local Indian group came to his defense and won his release, providing him food and shelter, but the rangers took the bow and arrows he had used for hunting. He wears army surplus pants, coat and boots and a medicine pouch around his neck. In the eyes of the gathering he is suspect number one. Naturally he finds his way to our gathering on the rocks.

He joins us on guitar and demonstrates an affinity for the immortal Jimi Hendrix. Between songs and musical passes we exchange stories. It seems the rangers will not allow him to proceed on his hike until the shooting is resolved. His journey has taken him through the desert and I ask him if he has seen Don Juan. He replies, without a smile: I am Don Juan.

An elderly couple emerges from a cabin near our circle. He is clearly incensed. He almost makes it to his car when he erupts. He explains that he and his wife were trying to meditate when the noise of our trumpet lesson broke their concentration and disturbed their peace. He is particularly angry that it wasn't even music, just a scale.

It has been a good hour since the lesson and Wiz wonders why he didn't say something at the time. The woman explains that they knew how they would be greeted: A couple of old fogies who can't stand fun.

Don Juan offers to play them a song but that only further incites the man: Now you're being smart! He storms off to the lodge as we continue the discussion with the woman. We apologize but suggest they were wrong to presume that we had no manners and were incapable of basic consideration. Had they said something we certainly would have stopped. They are not aware of what has transpired during the night and the day following. We have been up for many hours and have lost track of time. To them it is early but to us it is not. Time and circumstance have led us to this place against our intentions.

We make peace with the woman but we have lost our desire to make music.

I believe the old man is in danger. To feel such rage and be unable to conceive another way of diffusing it is unhealthy. What is the purpose of his meditations if not to handle these situations in a healthy manner? The Zen masters would welcome the distraction as a test of their powers of concentration. Embrace it and focus even deeper on the center of your being. If you cannot, seek remedy. Do not allow anger to control you. Do not bring yourself to rage. Or if you must, then understand it as belonging to you, take ownership and learn to find another way. Of course, we are not Zen masters so we do what we can.

We pack away the instruments and discuss our options. We study the road atlas for an alternative that might have escaped us. There is none. Wiz opens the Zen of Golf at random and reads: Be still and take in the breadth and depth of your surroundings.

The message is clear. I had been leaning the other way. The thought that keeps circling my mind is one that I do not allow myself to speak for fear of prophecy – like the prophecy of the pass closing: If we don't get out of California today, we never will. I should not allow my anxiety and fear to guide my actions.

Wiz suggests that we take our wedges and a couple balls and shoot our way to nearby Lukens Lake, about three miles by the trail. He only recently purchased his wedge at a second hand store in Motown and is anxious to give it a test run. I agree to the idea; it is too bizarre to pass up.

Before we embark, Don Juan offers us some sage with the explanation that he offers it to all the musicians he crosses on the path. I am pleased to be included in the blessing and accept his offering. Wiz returns the favor by giving him a CD of his girlfriend's album, a project he recorded and produced. I offer some jerky. It is the best I can do.

I later think: I should have given him my script for a play entitled: *The Ringed Women of the Sacred and Forbidden Forest.* It is the story of a hero's journey, inspired by Joseph Campbell. Maybe it would have been presumptuous. A journeyman must learn by his own lessons and experience.

We bid him farewell, uncertain that we will see him

again. We have formed a brotherhood and I believe he will remember us as we will remember him. A person can travel this country a thousand times and never meet a man as memorable as this man. He is Don Juan. It is a rare and special blessing.

We begin the hike by placing our balls at the foot of the trail. According to plan, we each have two balls and are determined to play them all the way to the lake. I am not aware that Wiz has tucked away a third ball for safe measure.

The first part of the trail is relatively wide and flat, allowing us to strike the ball with full swings, blasting away at fifty to seventy yards a shot. As we cross a creek the trail narrows, becomes rocky and climbs more steeply. Soon we find ourselves assuming the characters of Dufus McGhee and Shivas MacDuff, Scottish masters of the elegant game, and we begin counting strokes. I take a sizeable lead but lose them as I take drops at the cost of a stroke, concerned that the rocks will mark my wedge.

We both hit into the woods and after a long search for our balls decide to exchange roles. He will look for mine and I will look for his. We reason that since we have not focused on the other's ball we will be forced to rely on a sixth sense: Zen. Within minutes we find both balls.

Wiz loses one in the tall grass and we abandon the search when we discover water below the grass. It is then that Wiz reveals he has another ball stashed away. I am convinced that is why he lost one. I have cautioned many a fledgling golfer not to carry a ball in his pocket, particularly when hitting over water. It represents doubt and even the smallest measure of doubt can affect the golf swing. The same holds true of using an old, tattered ball, in anticipation of the worst. The golf gods smell doubt and the water draws the ball like a magnet.

We cross the path of some amazed hikers who tell us we are near the lake. Wiz is reluctant to give up his search. He has made it a goal to play the same ball all the way. It is hard to give up on your goals.

We finally resume the climb and Wiz overtakes me by two strokes as the lake suddenly appears before us. We observe golf etiquette and I am away. It is my shot. If it makes it to the lake through the trees, he will have two shots to win. I hit a beauty that finds an opening and sails into the middle of the lake. Wiz plays a set up shot to position himself. We agree that the next shot must enter the water from above rather than rolling in on the ground for his victory to be untainted.

He sets up, takes the club back, and unleashes a glorious shot, high as the clouds, securing his long awaited victory. I shake his hand and assure him that the victory is real. We have played the game in its best tradition and I have discovered there can be as much joy in losing well as there is in winning.

Wiz estimates we have played some three thousand shots on the trail to the lake. It has consumed nearly four hours – the length of a golf round. We begin our descent with our clubs tucked under our arms and the same self-satisfied feeling one has after a fine round on the course.

Wiz breaks into a trot that soon turns into a run. I follow his lead, hitting my stride, effortless and free of restraint. We approach the creek and I wonder how he will negotiate it. I am in his hands now. He leads and chooses the path. He seems to accelerate and I follow through the maze with a blindfold. He takes great leaping strides, one after another, flying like a hawk. I hear a crack as a log gives way. He is down, sprawled out on a boulder in the creek, one foot dangling in the water. I manage to stop before the fall and wonder how I failed to come down on top of him.

He looks up and I can tell by his expression he is not hurt. He was protected by his faith and his natural relaxation at the moment of impact. Only his ego is bruised. It is the most glorious fall I've ever seen but my smile does not comfort him [5]. He seems to perceive the event as a personal failing. I hold a distinctly different point of view. The gods will not abide overconfidence.

Like so many things in life, it is a delicate balance. We must conquer fear and eliminate doubt if we are to perform any task at a high level but the moment we begin to feel infallible or superior to our fellow beings, the gods put us down a rung. As it relates to Wiz's fall, I wonder what might have happened had he made that jump across the creek. Would it have given him an unreasonable sense of confidence and led to some reckless act down the road with potentially tragic consequences?

He does not accept it, not yet, but I am certain that he received the lesson he needed though not the one he wanted. He wanted transcendence and an affirmation of his spiritual achievement. Instead he received a lesson in humility. As it is in life, so it is in golf.

We are back on the trail and soon, like Apache runners in the deserts of New Mexico, we find our pace and hold to it. We reach the lodge only to discover that nothing has changed. The suspect is still at large. The rangers have evacuated another village down the road. The wait continues.

We decide it is time to move on. We wish Don Juan well and head for the pass, hoping that it will open before us. We drive for many miles, climbing to an elevation of 9,000 feet before we are pulled over at a lookout station by Fairview Dome and Tuolumne Meadows. The view is spectacular. The sky is clear and recalls the blues of Maxfield Parrish. El Capitan towers in the distance. Surrounded by the huge granite mountains that form this land, I can't imagine a manhunt on this terrain. The hopelessness of the pursued is rivaled only by the hopelessness of the pursuers.

We linger in the glory and the beauty and the majesty and the grace of mother earth, trying to communicate our gratitude with the sweet sounds of music. A park ranger about our age and of similar spirit breaks from his station to join us. He's a musician. We talk, he plays a song and he updates us on the situation. It might be minutes; it might be days. We are no more than twenty or thirty miles from crossing the pass and resuming our eastward journey but it is not to be.

We turn back. We are not defeated. We are certain that our path has been chosen. I am grateful we are in agreement. He later tells me that he also has been visited by the same haunting thought that has trailed me since our detainment at Wolf Creek. Though it runs counter to the philosophy of the journey, we must get out of California tonight.

[5] I debated whether I should include this episode, knowing Wiz would prefer its omission, but I decided it was an important event in the journey.

16

SKY OF A MILLION STARS

Sky of a million stars
Light of a thousand years
Bless this solemn crossing
With sweet imaginings

    We retrace our path down Tioga Pass into the foothills, a sense of urgency taking hold of us both. It is bizarre to be moving once again toward the setting sun. The grade grows steeper as the road narrows and winds around a mountain adorned with purple bushes. As we reach Groveland the mountains gradually yield to rolling hills. This is the home of what was once my favorite course: Pine Mountain Golf and Country Club. Built around a lake, the course uses the natural lay of the land. Elevated tees and greens are the rule and the greens are as slick as billiard tables with slopes and undulations to challenge the finest putter.
    It is a course I have walked only once and never will again. The climb between greens and tees is too steep and the beauty is too great for labor. Golf at Pine Mountain has long since given way to the country club. The privatization of such beautiful layouts is a process that began at the peak of golf's popularity. Maybe it will run its course. Maybe not. I've never really felt

comfortable in the company of the privileged class and they've never felt comfortable in mine. People being people and in my estimation essentially good, it is a failing I hope one day to conquer.

The sun has descended, breaking into a dozen hues of golden orange, purple and red when we make the turn near Chinese Camp. This was the land of outlaw Joaquin Murrieta and his loyal companion, Three-Fingered Jack, where indentured Chinese immigrants were quartered. They performed the dangerous and backbreaking work of cutting through the granite mountains of the Sierras to pave the way for Manifest Destiny. Anyone who has traveled these mountains is awed by what they did. It ought to be one of the seven wonders of the world.

To us it brings the startling reality that we are now no more than forty miles from where we began thirty-six hours ago. We might have walked as far. Wiz suggests that we return to Motown just for the look on their faces. I am too driven to take the bait and not completely sure he is joking.

We've got to get out of this place.

Once again we start the ascent to the high ground of the Sierra Nevada, Sonora Pass to the Devil's Gate. Darkness brings a chill as we roll in to Sonora, tired but not beaten.

We pull up at a restaurant on the far side of town. It's a nice place with white tablecloths, folded linen napkins and a spacious dining room. The waitress is about the age of Wiz's mom. She's a country music fan and assumes we are the same after we tell her we live in Nashville. We order steaks and enjoy the most gratifying meal of our journey. Suddenly we are not in a hurry. We gulp down as much coffee as we can hold and engage the waitress in a dialogue about her favorite music stars. We leave her a generous tip, Wiz leaves one of Rhonda's CD's, and hit the highway refreshed and renewed.

It's very late and there is no moon in the cloudless sky. We crawl to the top of Sonora Pass where we are compelled to pull over. I have been in these mountains countless times but never have I seen a sky so close and so teeming with stars and shining planets. It is bursting with cosmic energy: The sky of a million stars.

The power is so immense that like the canyon it tempts my soul to walk the stairway to heaven. The sky sings to us in a chorus of infinite voices. I now know the wonder of the muses and the pull of the graces in perfect harmony. Breathless, mesmerized and enthralled. There are no words. This glorious view is the reason there is music in the universe. There are no words.

We cannot stay long. We embrace the moment and

implant the image in our memories. It will last a lifetime. If we linger too long in this heavenly perfection we will never return to our earthly stations. We will wander like blind men in the valley of desolation. We will find no peace or consolation. If we linger too long we will go over the edge. We are not ready for such a destiny. It is not our time. It is a moment of inspiration, not of attainment.

We descend with the caution and respect the mountain demands. We walk a tightrope over an infinite void yet our spirits are light. We have been to the mountain. We have seen the playground of the gods. Now my human drive returns and presses on.

We come to a fork known as the Devil's Gate and veer south still on the California side of the Sierras. We enter a strange land where the human spirit is not welcome. It is a land of military installations, one after another, seemingly without end, devoid of hope. It is a land of death. We press on with the high of Sonora Pass, still fresh in our minds, protecting us from despair.

Wiz asks my consent to fall asleep and I give it to him. He knows I will soon need relief. At any other time on our journey I would pull over to rest but I need to drive on, to cross the border into Nevada. This mountain driving has sapped my strength and distorted my vision. The road now appears as if in a tunnel surrounded by thick layers of mist. Fog where there is no fog. Clouds in a cloudless sky.

We finally turn east, heading for Highway 6 across Nevada. If it were daytime we would be able to see the peaks of Tioga Pass not far away by the flight of the crow. I'm too tired to think and too exhausted to appreciate the irony. Wiz wakes up and senses my state of disorientation. He takes the wheel and we drive on.

As tired as I am, I am unable to sleep. I am beyond fatigue. I am in a state of suspended consciousness where no thoughts or visions outside the immediate are allowed. The road seems cold and unforgiving. Wiz is driving Sally hard. She seems to be flying as we hit a long series of undulations in the road. They are too small to be described as hills and much too large to be called bumps. Wiz wonders at a thumping sound each time we roll over an undulation. I tell him it's the sound of Sally hitting bottom. He slows down. He is far-gone. We both are.

It seems an eternity before we cross the state line. At last we are free to express our mutual fear of never escaping the grip of California. A strange mood overtakes us, a sense of accomplishment and rebirth in the high desert plains of Nevada. We've finally made it. We pull over and sleep until dawn.

We awaken in a different world, the chill of night carrying over to morning light. It is stunning how radically the land changes on the Nevada side of the Sierras. Each state is distinct as if the boundaries are laid more by nature than by politics. Nevada is the land of sagebrush and coyotes, the land of the crow and barren flatlands. If you wanted to capture desolation you would picture the land before us.

Our next destiny is Boulder, Colorado. Our route will take us through Nevada and Utah. It is a mirror image of our westward journey, beginning to the south on Highway 6 and crossing over to the north at St. Louis, Missouri. The two paths intersect at only one point: Eli, Nevada.

What first appeared to us as an oasis on a desperate

stretch of road now appears as a crossroads, a place where the highways converge from all directions. It is a fitting place for a round of golf.

First we pay a visit to the local Burger King for coffee and breakfast. The pickup in front of us has the inexplicable numbers 666 on its license plate. Imagine being so immune to humanity's obsession with numbers and religion that you would drive a vehicle with that designation. It appears to be a company truck and I don't know what to make of it.

An attractive Hispanic woman at the drive-through window is exceptionally friendly. She comments on the instruments in the back and gives us extra sugar and cream with a smile. I enjoy the image of traveling musicians. Wiz suggests this might not be such a bad place to settle down. I let it pass without comment but it leads me to wonder what life is like in a place like this. Why would anyone choose this of all places given the beauty we have seen on our journey? Heaven is where the heart leads and I suppose even this could be heaven with the right person and the right state of mind. But why here? The promise of employment is the only answer.

There is a convention of golfers at a local motel. The sign reads: Welcome, Golfers! That is a sign we know what to do with. On our stop for gas, Wiz opens the hood and discovers a problem. The six-inch bolt that holds the alternator in place has broken. If not replaced it will drain the battery and leave us stranded. It is only a matter of time. The guy at the station shakes his head and directs us to a shop outside of town. We decide to let it ride for now. It's early in the day and we have a yen for golf.

We look up the local course and sign up for a round

of nine. The course is flat with sparse trees and the fairways are hard as stone. We hit a bucket of balls before the round and it reminds me of how weary I am. The road can remove your sense of grounding. This round will be about balance. The first lesson of Zen Golf: Without balance there is nothing.

We play well on a course that is as simple and uninspired as a landfill. The holes resemble each other to the extent that in the middle of the round we tee off on the wrong hole. It is not until we walk to our drives that we realize we have played this hole before: déjà vu. Ironically, it is my best drive of the day, a soaring 300-yard shot down the right side of the fairway.

As we pick up our balls and reorient, a twosome behind us catches up and we invite them to play through. They accept and take the tee. They look like businessmen, one of whom is a large man who carries an extra long, graphite shaft, maximum distance driver with an oversized metal head. Inevitable as they may be, these new drivers bother me. I understand the role of technology in the advancement of the game and I have no desire to go back to wooden shafts, the knobby and the baffle. But there is something unsavory about these new drivers and balls that allow a common player to simulate the power of a professional. They do not encourage the beauty and creativity of the swing. The long shaft forces a flat trajectory that usually involves a hitch in the backswing. It's not a pretty thing to watch and the golfer who buys into the power game will soon be lost.

The big man hits a solid drive down the middle and struts after it with a satisfied smile, ignoring our compliments. He is challenging the gods. I wait for them to clear and send a rocket in their wake. They look back in acknowledging a cold fact: the skinny guy with a persimmons wood has out-driven the big man with the high-tech equipment.

My flirtation with the power game has a predictable and immediate impact. The gods have delivered a lesson in humility to the big man; now they turn in my direction. I have forgotten the essential lesson of the day: Balance. Focus. Finding the center. I struggle to finish the round, grinding against the wind, and we head back to Sally. It is close to five o'clock so we decide to check out the mechanic's shop on the outskirts of town.

Once again Wiz takes the lead. He has a gift for these interactions. He teaches me a lot about making connections with an array of people. With reference to auto mechanics he has a great deal of knowledge and tells me knowing the language is critical.

He never begins with business. He makes small talk: How ya doing? Nice country you got here. The manager tells us this is the first day in a long while the wind has settled down. Across the country, in the Midwest, a relentless storm has swelled the Missouri and Mississippi Rivers to record depths. Here the wind whips the dry land into a dust bowl.

It is closing time but Wiz engages the man in conversation, inviting him to play a round, describing the course in favorable terms. The manager passes on the offer but it is clear he takes a liking to Wiz. He asks if anyone would be willing to put in some overtime to repair Sally and the man agrees. It's a tricky job but he's up to it. It takes him about half an hour and the fee he charges is more than reasonable.

Wiz leaves a couple of CD's and we head out across the ancient red rock lands of Utah, with its cave dwellings and towering carved stone monuments, a Stonehenge of nature. Despite its infinite beauty, Utah has no specific attraction for us. We drive the interstate and watch the land, its changes in texture, color and feel. We observe the now frequent appearances of crow in murders of five to seven. They have mastered this territory and rule over it as a baron would his estate. To us it is a place of silent contemplation, communion with the spirit world, and unity with the earth.

We reach Colorado by nightfall and press on to Glenwood Springs. We give up the push to reach Boulder and settle in for the night. Checking in at a roadside motel, we shower and shake the road from our bones. For the first time in weeks it seems we have a little time. I check out some baseball on the tube. The Giants are in first place and all is right in the world.

I feel a sudden surge of energy and suggest we hit the streets. Wiz is for once reluctant but he follows my lead. We hit the liquor store down the street where we purchase a fifth of brandy, a couple of ales and two samplers of Mescal con Dos Gusanos. Two worms each. We check out a place that's supposed to have live music but it's not happening. The door is locked. We take it as a sign. We don't need action so much as to go looking for it. Not tonight. We have a meal at an all-night diner, head back to the motel, kick off our shoes, click on the TV and try to make a dent in the booze we've bought. One hit of brandy and half an ale and we're both out for the night. The spirit is willing but the body is not. So be it.

We are awakened in morning by a knock at the door. Our plan for an early departure is gone. It's close to ten thirty and the maid wants to finish her rounds. We wave her off and go about our morning routine. In no mood to hurry, I run over to the office for coffee, doughnuts and a newspaper. We click on the tube and are greeted by *Buffy the Vampire Slayer*. It's a kick in the ass. Wiz rearranges the packing in Sally and we stretch out our departure past check out. The maid will have to wait. Buffy has captured us and we hold out to the end. A Paul Ruben death scene, milked relentlessly, gives us fits of laughter. It feels good to laugh.

Whatever spirit looks over us, it is smiling upon us today. It's a great day for driving, a great day for sitting in the sun, a great day for laughter, playing music, singing and being alive. We are the last car in the parking lot. The maid smiles. She thinks we must be high and I think she must be right. We have a good breakfast and head out well rested and bound for glory in a place called Boulder.

Beyond Grand Junction there is a stretch of highway that extols the meeting of the Rocky Mountains and the Colorado River. To the first roaming tribes of North America or the first European pioneers, this land must have seemed a Mecca, a promised land, a land of the gods and goddesses, a land of blessed enchantment. Now it is a Mecca for tourists. The place smells of avarice, rich and bittersweet like unsweetened chocolate. Vail is down the highway and Aspen is due south.

Around Grand Junction the highway is under construction. Fresh corpses of deer and other wildlife are common on the roadside. Signs warn that eagles land on this stretch of road. What on this green earth would lead the great bird of the North American continent to land on a busy interstate? Is this sacred land? Is it a protest of human encroachment? I believe that tourism is to the natural inhabitants of the land what the invasion of Jesuits was to the indigenous tribes. It promises the blessings of prosperity but it brings inevitable ruin. In the end nothing will be spared the onslaught.

At first we resist the temptation to mingle with the wealthy, driving by the first roadside golf course, a beautifully manicured layout at the base of the Rockies in this narrow interstate valley. I tell Wiz I know them. I know their kind. It is a prejudice I have learned over the years. They don't like our kind around.

Wiz is not convinced and my resistance breaks down when we approach another course. Wiz wants to check it out. Why not? What have we got to lose? I pull off the freeway and pull in to tourist land. It is a maze of social activity. Summer vacation condos form its center and a bar at its base overlooks the golf course. Outside a yuppie adolescent crowd plays mud volleyball to the tune of rock and roll. There is something odd and comical about their willingness to get down and dirty. Some seem less adapted than others. They take the pose and look the part but are willing to go no farther than a step in any direction. Their less restrained comrades are in it from head to toe: the mud people of Gypsum.

It seems to me they are the same make as us. The only thing that separates us is their parents' bank accounts. We represent the working class and they fear us. They believe we want what they have. We do not. We desire something of far greater worth. We want what they want and what money cannot buy: Peace, freedom, wisdom, enlightenment. We have more in common than they realize.

Our first stop is at the driving range where a lesson

is in progress. They are among the worst golfers I have ever seen. The lesson is antithetical to Zen: all nuts and bolts. Keep the left arm straight, tuck the right elbow in, fix the shoulder under the chin and keep your head down. It is the golf of restraint. Avoid errors and all will be well. A left-handed golfer stands apart and strikes a contrast. He sends shots that rise and soar like a glider and set down like a ball of cotton. He is a Zen golfer. They take no notice. He is not one of them but he has adapted to their presence. The lesson is private and we are directed to the clubhouse.

I know at a glance it is overpriced. We talk to a uniformed employee outside the clubhouse and she gives us the lowdown: Tee times are booked in advance, the price is high and includes carts. Walking is not allowed. We politely protest that walking is a part of the game. She's sure we're right but she's not a golfer. This is not our place.

We hang a while, have a beer and observe the yuppie gathering. It is not our place.

Returning to Sally, I give her a crank but she stutters and stalls. At length Wiz pulls the air filter and she finally starts. It seems the combination of thin air and low octane gas has deprived her of essential oxygen. She is choking to death. I promise her a jump in octane at the next gas station and we head out. We are haunted by a sense of not belonging. We need to be welcome. We need a place with familiar signs and warm memories. We need to be where the people know and embrace us for who we are and such a place looms ahead.

17

BOULDER, COLORADO

The last time I saw Boulder I was eighteen and a draft fugitive. Had I known it at the time I might not have enjoyed it so much. I had just completed my first season of summer theater and linked up with a fellow actor who wanted to return home to York, Pennsylvania. We lost a loved one that memorable summer. Mary was the stage manager for a production of *Man of La Mancha*. She walked out of a rehearsal and was struck by an eighteen-wheeler. She never regained consciousness.

I still remember her smile. The charm and love of life she possessed filled my soul with a warm and tender feeling I did not fully understand. She captured the beauty of innocence. My friend Tony had dated her while I had only dreamed of her. We both mourned her passing. It was my first real encounter with death and it cut deep into my soul.

Tony was a talented singer. He had the voice of Anthony Newley from *The Roar of the Greasepaint, The Smell of the Crowd*. He had ridden his thumb cross-country more than once. He despised the southern route. I had seen *Easy Rider* but I never asked him why. Though summer had ended and a cold wind would be coming soon, we opted for the northern route:

Interstate 80 to Reno, Winnemucca, Salt Lake City, Cheyenne, Omaha, Chicago and Cleveland. We were stranded for seventeen hours at the off-ramp to Mustang, Nevada, a location notable only for its world famous brothel. Some drunken fool with a twisted sense of humor dropped us there. We didn't have the kind of money we needed to go inside so we waited along the narrow, two-lane highway until we finally realized that no-one would pick up a couple of guys outside a whore house.

We decided to walk. The problem was he wanted to walk back to Reno and I wanted to walk east. It was a conviction I had by instinct and hold to this day: Never turn back. Destiny lies ahead.

We started walking separate ways, a chip on both our shoulders, before he relented and caught up to me. Within half an hour a trucker picked us up. In those days that was a miracle. We had a hierarchy of expectations when it came to hitching. Volkswagen busses were on the top of everyone's list and diesel trucks were on the bottom. It was against company policy. In all my days of hitching that was the only time a trucker gave me a ride.

He let us off in Winnemucca, a place of infinite desolation. We spent some time reading notes of desperation scribbled and scratched on the road sign. We were more fortunate. A guy with a camper on the back of his pickup stopped and asked us if we could drive a standard transmission. He was headed for Ohio and needed drivers. We told him we could, no problem, and we climbed aboard.

He checked us out for a while, decided we were okay, and climbed in the back to sleep. We got off the interstate and sailed down the highway at an average speed between sixty-five and seventy. We slept in shifts. I was at the wheel when we came across a couple of fellow hitchhikers in the Cowboy State of Wyoming. We could see their spirits rise as they checked our appearance. We were brethren but all we could do was shrug and gesture, trying to convey our predicament, as they waved frantically and threw their sign and then their bags in the road as we drove by.

Like the stalled fellow travelers on the loneliest road in America, it stayed with me and made me question my character. Maybe we should have stopped but it wasn't our place. More than likely we would have joined them on the side of the road when our sleeping vehicle owner woke up. No one can say what might have happened. We came to a crossroad and we made a choice.

We crossed the Mississippi at night and made it to Chesapeake Bay the following day. The entire crossing took only two and a half days. I spent a week with Tony's parents. He was their only child and they were grateful for his return. They treated me as a welcome guest. I remember clearly the most prized possession of their home: a framed photograph of his father and John Wayne on the mantle of their fireplace. Both wore navy uniforms. These were hard working people with basic values and a wandering son they did not quite understand. I connected and respected their ways though I knew I was only a passing stranger. It was not my place.

From York I headed north to New Hampshire where I fell in love with autumn. I had never seen a display of colors more beautiful outside the realms of art and imagination. Hills covered with multi-colored trees in magnificent bloom. The way they blended in perfect harmony reminded me of the impressionists: Monet, Renoir and the like. I spent the better part of two weeks there, communing with nature and visiting a friend from home. I had known Janis since grade school though we had never been close. I felt like Thoreau at Walden Pond.

As the north wind blew in and brought a chill to the bone, I departed with a promise to return. Two decades later I have not kept that promise though I have often returned in my heart and mind.

On the journey home I was invited to join a theater company in Lincoln, Nebraska, but the pull of home was far too strong. I had a written invitation to audition for the renowned Guthrie Theater in Minnesota but the road was long and the wind ever colder. I wonder as we all must wonder what might have happened had I made a different choice. How might my life be altered had I stayed in Lincoln or ventured north to Minnesota? Don't look back.

I fell in love with Boulder on that journey. The people were open and kind to wandering strangers. They seemed enlightened, bright eyes in a land of dull faces. I spent only two days there, sleeping in the dormitory lounge at the university until security rousted me in the morning, but it left an enduring impression.

I arrived home in Modesto, kicking up my heels alongside the road to the amusement of passing cars, only to discover that I was already a month late in reporting for my draft physical. Knowing it would not be approved, my family not being church-going Christians, I had written a radical application for conscientious objector status. My oldest brother, John, had already distinguished himself by refusing to step forward at his induction ceremony. Following his example, I had read a book called *4F* and decided my best shot was to starve myself so I would be under the minimum weight requirement. I had done so. Even on the road I had limited my meals to salads, soups and crackers. I recall a woman palming me a twenty-dollar bill at a restaurant. She thought I was starving.

When I reported to the draft center in Fresno they instructed us to hold our clothes in our arms as we were weighed. I don't know if that was the usual procedure or if they saw me coming and knew what I intended. Instead of below the weight guideline it put me just above. In the infamous bend-over room made famous by Arlo Guthrie in *Alice's Restaurant* I heard a doctor comment on how skinny I was. An attendant replied that I was over the requirement.

When it was over the prospective inductees for the next shipment to Nam were assembled in a holding room and called one-by-one for our final conferences. The order was alphabetical until they came to me. They saved me for last. I entered the small conference room and the doctor in charge called all of his associates into the room. There could be no doubt I was being treated differently.

"Look at this guy," the head doctor says. "Do you think he could make it through basic training?"

"Depends on how much he wants it."

"He doesn't want it."

I was a little stunned by the proceedings but I nodded in agreement. I didn't want it. Regardless of their actions, I would not enter the military and I would not go to their war.

At the end, the man in charge says: "You may get a notice in the mail that you're 1-A but don't worry, you won't get called."

I don't know why but I believed him. Maybe they had made a simple calculation and decided I was more trouble than I was worth or maybe they knew something I didn't know: President Richard Nixon was about to call off the draft.

The fact is I was never called and was not called upon to refuse induction. That distinction belonged to my brother John and I will always honor him for it.

That was my first cross-country journey. It was filled with wonders and trials and crossroads with the power to change my life. The choices I made then have made me who I am today.

We drive into town, memories of a sacred place sifting through our minds. We stop for gas and I ask the clerk what's happening while Wiz attends to Sally. She doesn't know about golf. She doesn't know about the Shakespeare Festival. She doesn't know about jazz. But when I ask about the poetry scene her eyes light up. She tells me where it's happening and when. She says Alan Ginsberg is in town teaching a class at the Institute.

Wiz checks the phone book for the nearest course and our plan takes shape. First we golf in the shadow of the Rockies, then we perform on the streets of Boulder and, finally, we check out the recommended poetry café.

The golf course is strikingly beautiful, more for its surroundings than for its design. It is the new breed of courses, the centerpiece of a housing development. The layout is long, its fairways contoured and well tended, and its greens are smooth, fast and sloped. The round promises to be challenging.

We are paired with an older couple, good and solid people. The man uses an iron off the tee and rarely gets the ball off the ground. We learn he is recovering from back surgery. His wife is a beginner but she has a better natural swing than her husband. With a little instruction (for example, hit down to get the ball up) they could be good golfers but they don't seem to mind. They enjoy the round despite their games.

Wiz and I play our normal games. We have some difficulty reading the break and speed of the greens. On the sixth hole I hit a solid three-wood off the tee and stiff an eight-iron within ten feet of the pin. The putt is true, dead solid and center of the cup. I look up with a smile and immediately recall the bargain we have struck: After the next birdie, we eat the worm. In this case, it's two worms each: Dos Gusanos.

We carry our mescal samplers in our bags for just this occasion. The next hole is a long par three to an elevated green. We tee off and linger to allow our playing partners to move ahead. They would not approve. We whip out our little samplers and down them in a gulp.

I am amazed at how well I play under the influence of the worm. The world beneath the world opens to my eyes. Don Juan howls in the breeze and hovers over my shoulder. Our partners are like family to us. On the ninth hole we share stories, share confidences and depart with heartfelt warm wishes.

Boulder is a magical mystery tour.

Our spirits soaring, we head downtown primed for music, jazz and poetry. Wiz leads us to the town square at the beginning of a pedestrian street where motor vehicles and bad tidings are not allowed. We park Sally and walk down the pedestrian street where performers of all stripes set up shop. We come upon a couple of bongo players and a gypsy dancer. In the flash of a moment I know her. I have always known her. She is a dream I have dreamed. She is the love I have always held in my heart. She is the queen of the gypsies: Esmeralda.

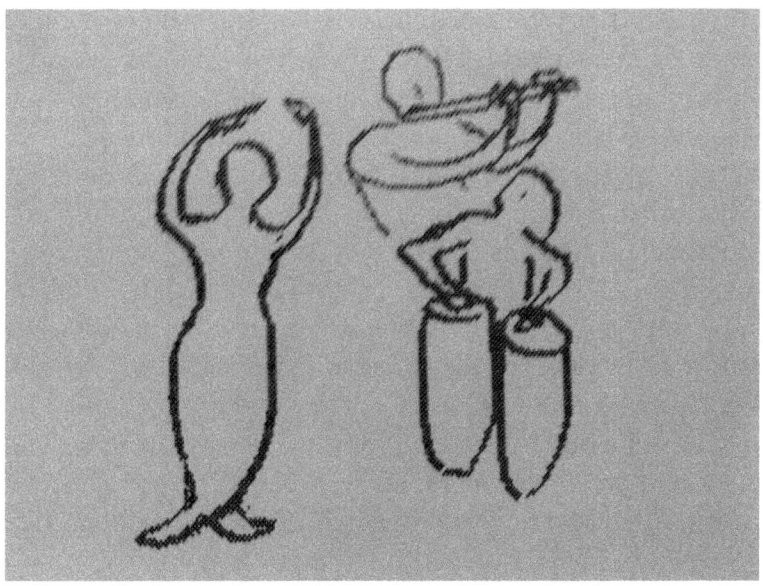

I pull out pen and notebook and begin to write, looking up only to gather the inspiration that comes with each breath, each wave of music and each turn of the gypsy's dance. Wiz joins the musical feast and it charges the dance of the gypsy like a fresh breeze, like the first taste of ocean air, like the first glimpse of Grand Canyon. The enchanted circle grows. The words come faster than I am able to write. I must slow them, deceive them, charm them to then capture them.

They are as illusive as a gypsy's love.

The music gradually descends from its high perch to the solid earth and the dancer lets go the dream and surrenders to waking movement. The players converse as actors do between scenes at a rehearsal. They shake hands with Wiz. He passes the audition. My words finally run dry, as if they were carried by the music and the dance and when the music and the dance ceased the words emptied in the wake.

I join them in the circle and Wiz introduces me as a poet of the streets. He suggests we join forces and it causes a surprising split. One of the percussionists is reluctant and skeptical and he communicates his opinion with a scowl and a sarcastic wit. He does not wish to share the stage. The gypsy dancer has already encroached on his territory and stolen much of his thunder, as gypsies will. He has not conceded to allow Wiz and his magic flute yet already he is asked to embrace a poet of the streets. Maybe he has trouble recognizing my art form.

I might have been offended but it only amused me. I've had my own share of trouble recognizing my art form. I have no need to recite my words aloud. I'm pleased to have captured them on paper.

The other bongo player – no doubt the wiser – strikes a different chord with a smile that spreads good tidings to match a mood of joyous celebration. He welcomes all artists of the street. He recognizes an enchanted moment and answers with a recitation of a poem he has committed to memory. His words punctuate and hang in the air like a lingering melody of strings. It is an invitation and a challenge. This is the standard to which my words will be held. I nod and smile. I understand his message and I like his style. I have made no decision to read or not to read.

The next round of music and dance begins. I wait to catch the wave. Not any wave will do. Just as each wave requires a different style of surfing, each rhythm calls for a different style of poetry. I don't do country, folk, rock or Irish. Give me jazz, blues or space jam and I'll begin to dance.

I wait and listen but mostly I watch the dance and the dancer. Her eyes are mystical and her movement has the grace of divinity. At length, the spirit enters my soul and I jump on the next wave.

A karmic debt is mounting like invaders at the shore
Another land to conquer
Another face to scorn
With every tick of the cosmic clock
Another soldier off to war

The rhythm builds and changes like the wind before a storm. It carries me like a dream of flight among the stars.

Speak no more of troubled times
Days of mourning
Dawns of no tomorrow
Hear no more the winds of darkness spreading woe
Unloading tears of sorrow

Heaven lives upon the earth to those who care to find it
Angels line the clouds and wait their turns
The garden is the earth
What more could heaven be?

Hell hath no choice

In heaven we are free
Free to choose the darkness or the light
Free to choose the battles we will fight

My love is my heaven here and now
Speak no more of bring me down
And suffer me to truth
I love therefore I am the truth
And love is my master

The gypsy soars to a higher plain and moves me to the core and center of my being, like the hand of Ariel upon my brow. I offer the only gratitude I have to give.

Esmeralda on the streets of Boulder
Spinning at the center of all life
Eyes dancing with fire rage desire
Soul tempting ecstasy
Forces of an ancient wind howl
And move this precious jewel beyond words
Beyond passion and beyond the edge of reason
The body as an instrument of faith finely tuned
To raise the lightning rod that dwells within
The sacred soul of self
Blast me with the fuel of your undaunted devotion
Pure and unpolluted by the hand of social righteousness
Fear not the wagging tongues and bulging eyes of
Those who cannot walk the streets with open shirts
You are the wind the blessed child of mother earth
The chosen of the nameless flock that follow their noses
To the maze of mindless wonder and dumbstruck awe
And settle in the circle of their own misery
Content and comfortably numb
You are the object of their desires

They dream of you and pray to meet you in another life
Dance and let the masses dream
Sweet nectar of life be yours to embrace
And ours to behold

What are words to their inspiration when the inspiration is itself inspired? They linger and hesitate as if awaiting her sacred blessing. They rise like puffs of smoke and scatter with a passing breeze. Today they have hit the mark, a standard far greater than the lofty verse of my challenger. They do not require approval. They have spoken to the moment, honest and true. If poetry is an oral tradition I feel I have discovered its essence. This is the method of the true street poet, immediate and engaging, inspired by the real world in motion. Still, I await the words of my gypsy dancer and alas she speaks: *Wow*.

Though it is not poetic that one syllable is more gratifying than the most eloquent praise. It is as if she has awakened from a dream. She speaks in an airy distant voice and solves the moment's mystery: *That's beautiful*. Sweet fulfillment is mine. Sweet love of innocence is reborn. Her simple words have filled my heart with joy more faithfully than all the treasures of my youth. She embraces my song of praise.

She tells me her name is Rain Forest though from time to time she has answered to the name of Esmeralda. She asks if can have my poem and stops me as I start to tear the page from my notebook. She borrows my pen and copies the words in her own hand.

She tells me *The Hunchback of Notre Dame* is one of her favorite stories along with *Cyrano d'Bergerac*. I proclaim her a romantic and she returns the compliment. I tell her I am pleased there are still some of us left in the world. We don't speak of normal, ordinary things, our lives in the daily world. We know enough already. When we shook hands an electrical charge sealed our bond forever.

Some say – and who's to say it is not so – our lives are built on prior lives. I know her spirit and she knows mine. Might I have been Cyrano to her Roxanne or the unrequited poet to her Esmeralda? There are far stranger things in life than even our dreams allow. Tonight has been her debut on the streets of Boulder and a legend has been born.

She thanks me for the poem and I thank her for the dance. She thanks me again in the poetry of motion. This time she dances for me. My eyes are riveted to her body in flowing, writhing, floating and sensual motion. She taps an ancient consciousness. She transforms her perfect being into universal spirit. When her eyes meet mine there is a pull of energy so strong it renders me helpless. I am grateful to be sitting. If I were standing her power would have knocked me to the ground leaving me breathless and at her command.

The time has come for her to part. Like a mermaid in an ocean mist she will fade away into the streets of Boulder. She has a return date with the wiser of bongo players. The other has long departed. I wish her well as I watch her turn and walk away. She does not look back. I am not likely to see her again but her image is burned into my mind and the moment is eternal.

Wiz and I linger, enjoying the company of strangers and basking in the afterglow. We know something rare and memorable has happened. They resume playing a while longer. My words are spent but my spirit is alive with the creative force. We make a clean break and

wander down the pedestrian walkway, Wiz playing as we walk, refining his chops on his magic flute.
Everywhere we go he is greeted by smiles and receives compliments. They offer money. They ask him to stay and play. They thank him for a moment of surreal enchantment. Wiz is in his element. This city loves his instrument and he is a master masquerading as an apprentice. They recognize his gift.
Wiz speaks of the flute in relation to the cities he has played. He tells me New Orleans, birthplace of jazz, does not embrace the sound. He can make it cry and draw the tears of angels but it seems the Easy is too dark for such a heavenly sound. It is not the muse of vampires. Even a jazzman flautist might starve in New Orleans but here he would thrive.
We stroll down the enchanted boulevard, pausing here and there to breathe in enclaves of entertainment, jazz, rhythm and blues. Some rock and roll musicians stand alone, gathering contributions from passersby. Fiddlers draw a crowd. I notice that there are no poets on the streets – not even here in this sanctuary city of free expression. A juggler draws the largest gathering and receives thunderous applause for his performance. In the land of the enlightened, the fool is king.
A stunning woman in conservative dress and style approaches Wiz and then falls back. He waves her forward. She tells him she's in love with his silver flute. She's a devoted follower of Ian Anderson, also known as Jethro Tull. Wiz knows the style but he refuses to go there. He believes it is addictive and pushes away all other styles of play. But now, in her honor, he plays the patented chops that made Jethro Tull famous. She loves it and offers him money. He refuses and gives her a CD.

"Write to the address on the back," he says, "and I'll send you one of my own."

She thanks him again and we walk on. His following grows and another soul is lighter for his passing. Karma.

We grab a couple of falafels and sit where a trio of Blues Brother types is on break between sets. The bench where we're sitting has an overhang that blocks our view of the upper halves of their bodies. We notice that their shoes are not a good fit to their feet. They walk away. Their gig is up. With a tip of the hat we head out to find the poetry café.

We locate it a couple of blocks down from the pedestrian walk still on the main boulevard. It looks like a happening place and it's divided into two sections. The smaller section features an improvised stage consisting of two plywood sheets mounted on four-by-fours. Lighting is sparse and about thirty punk rockers crowd into a small audience area.

We gather that the poetry scene is not on the program tonight and shift to the larger section. It has the appearance of a gift shop with a bountiful stock of postcards, greeting cards, tee shirts and miscellaneous items. The place strikes me as a little off center, cool but in a designer way. As it happens I've been known to collect a few postcards for my heroes series so I give their stock a look: They have several of Geronimo, the Apache war chief who inherited his name from the Spanish soldiers that faced his revenge after slaughtering his family. They have Sarah Winnemucca, a famous Paiute educator and early Indian rights activist. They have a variety of native shaman, warriors and chiefs. They have the blues diva Bessie Smith, the immortal Marilyn Monroe, the inimitable

Mark Twain and Andy Warhol.

One card features "Bill and Al at the Democratic Convention" circa 1968. It's a photo of William Burroughs and Alan Ginsberg and it looks like they're trying to figure it out. I doubt they ever succeeded.

As we shuffle through the shop we notice a woman who seems to be stuck at the counter trying to carry a large metal machine of some type out to her car. She's clearly having a hard time with it. Quick on his feet and always a gentleman, Wiz moves to her assistance only to be greeted with a stern reprimand. Wiz takes a step back and we both watch her struggle with the task. She turns back at the door with the comment: *There's nothing I hate more than that.* It's all I can do not to reply: *How about serial killers?* I know she's trying to make a statement about women's rights and women's equality but this is neither the place nor the time.

Does she think Wiz or I would not offer to help if it was a man struggling with a heavy object? She is wrong, flat wrong, and she does not serve her cause. In fact she does it harm. We are her natural allies but she has made us her enemy.

It is far too typical of factions on the left of the political divide. We turn on our own. We divide against ourselves. Our true opposition – the status quo, the establishment, the power structure, the system – has no reason to fear us. Give us time and opportunity and we will destroy ourselves.

I gather a handful of postcards and take them to the counter where another woman informs me before I ask that they do not accept credit cards. I pay cash for the cards and a latte and ask for change to use in the postage stamp machine. She directs me to a Quick Stop down the road. This is not a friendly place. They want our money but they don't want us.

    We sit at a table at the front of the shop. I sit in a huge wood chair carved into the shape of a grizzly. I'm not usually that bold but this place raises my ire. I scope the scene and the reality of the place hits me like a jolt of Irish whiskey on a December morning. I focus on the taller of the two women behind the espresso counter: braless, mother earth style, attractive but detached and aloof. My vantage point allows me to scan the split scene in one take. Wiz heads out to create his own scene while I whip out my notebook and write.

Slick circle of lesbian dreams
She practices at being hip so long the mirror cracks
Late sixties dress clean lean
And hanging from her pointed nipples by a thread
Don't look she says with eyes that shoot missiles
Cool, baby blue, I can take you at a moment's glance
And leave you breathless like a slow dance
That grooves so long it steals the light from romance
Bend baby shake it down and grab the inner beast
Your soul be mine to shine and glorify
Or bury like a busted toaster rust and turn to dust
Smile baby blue your eyes are meant to grow
The morning light not down the midnight high
There is no train but this we ride together
There is no truth we cannot lie
Break down the walls that vilify
I see you dancing in blue moonlight
Thunder rain and heaven's flight
I see your perfect soul unleashed in dreams
Of raw desire
I see your hunger filled in rhapsodies
And waves of come and come again

I see your slender body open like a broken dam
And rush whitewater crash and burn
Implode in pulsing grace
I see your love lust and tender mercy
Hide your root and center core
Emerge the raging fire Eros
Radiate in sultry light
You and I are lovers from a million lives
Before this hallowed crossing
I greet you with a kiss and praise your sheltered beauty
Awaken and steal the breath of sunlight
This wine will last forever

I cannot abide the separatism and exclusivity of the new minorities. The lesbian left begins to appear as bigoted as the old boy south or the south side of Boston or the country clubbers of Pine Mountain or the yuppies of Veil and Aspen. Having felt the weight of oppression they seek to impose it on innocent others. Is a man required to join their club to walk amongst them, to know their humanity and feel the basic link that ties us all together? It is a strange and foolish phenomenon. It enables the righteous right to strike them down. When the hammer comes looking they will reach for the hands of friends and allies they've discarded. Who then will stand with them? In the hour of need pray that we will find a way to forgive and stand as one.

Our differences are not so great yet the breach of trust, the betrayals large and small, have so widened the gaps between us that they begin to appear as vast as Grand Canyon under the light of a full moon. When will we make an end? When will we find a way?

I finish my scribe as a wild and writhing dancer appears before me as if by divine will. The gig is on and I cannot stop my pen.

> *Shake it baby grind and waste the pining light*
> *Jazz be yours in major jam and chase the dying night*
> *Snake and move the heavens to align*
> *Rise the pulsing heat of all and ever force of life*
> *Jazz be yours and mated with desire*
> *Tap the caveman down and dirty*
> *Lava flows in endless rolls of joy and madness*
> *Dive the ancient pools of Mother Nature's womb*
> *Jazz be yours and slide the stream of want and dream*
> *And sink to endless heights*
> *Down and down again the depths of core desire*
> *Sweet blue flame of falling over edge of sane*
> *And Dionysus mourning*
> *Heat and fold the waterfalls of time*
> *Jazz be yours to hold and mine to delight*

We head back through the pedestrian walkway, our spirits thriving, Wiz playing flute and me reading intermittently. Wiz discovers a sign that our path is true. There beneath the bench where we sat to hear the Blues Brothers trio is a pair of shining patent leather shoes. Having heard our musing one of them must have left this offering in lieu of their music. Wiz tries them on: a perfect fit.

We continue our stroll back to Sally feeling good about ourselves and the world that surrounds us. A university student at an outdoor table of a beer bar offers Wiz five bucks to play. He turns down the five but plays for his amusement. We end up inside where another student tells us Boulder is a doomed city. He explains that it lies on a flood plain and it's only a matter of time before it's swept away.

I imagine being a Californian trying to escape the big earthquake or an Oklahoman escaping tornado alley, coming to Boulder only to be swept away by a great flood. There is no escape. We can only accept the dangers that confront us and live.

He is a student of literature but he doesn't write. He doesn't believe he has the talent. His favorite writer is Dickens and his favorite novel *A Tale of Two Cities*. He appears to be a typical football and Friday night college student, like the dandies of Vandy in Nashville, but he has a lot to offer in a world desperately in need. Appearances can deceive.

It is almost midnight and we are content with our Boulder experience. We offer our thanks and move on. Within a block of Sally a corner full of activity inspires Wiz to a final improvisational performance. He draws a crowd that includes a raggedy man with wild eyes who praises him to the heavens. The man is awed by Wiz's three-foot silver flute and the sound he creates with it. He asks if he can play it.

This is new ground. In all the time I have known Wiz no one has asked to play his prized instrument. To my surprise he allows the man to play a few riffs. He returns the instrument to its owner and invites him to join him for a few songs down the street. Within minutes we are back at the corner where we began this adventure. They set up in a waiting station for public transit that resembles a plastic bubble and begin to play. It turns out he's a talented Irish-Indian-Mexican flamenco guitarist. He's looking to make a comeback. He had founded an Irish folk group that broke apart after a brief period of success. He has visions of a new group combining his talents with Wiz.

My writing muse still burning, I let their music take

me where it will. I write without thought, without care and without the editor that stops the flow. I ride the wave for all it's worth knowing it is a moment that does not happen every day.

City of a thousand boundless dreams
Police sirens at the crack of midnight
Don Juan on flamenco guitar
Soul of the flute blazes the wind
Scorching the Boulder skyline
City of melodies that never sleep
Dancing in perfect harmony
To the beat of higher consciousness
Heartbeats cruise the upper maze
Ground the flight of angels
Scream the stream of rising flight
Coyote on the run
Raven perched on sacred heights
Gray hawk soars on Navaho winds
Pierce the secret soul of wisdom grace and glory
Muse like the first flight of butterflies
Shower me with blessings
Rare and precious jewels to fuel the flames
Of sweet and sacred visions
Lore of the ancient tribe of wanderers
Thought of the first philosopher
Rhyme of the virgin poet
Breath of the first ocean breeze
Beauty rises from the barren depths
To nourish the forest of harmony
And give birth to a singular truth:
We are one with all and all is one within

Hours have passed in moments. The Irish Indian

has made his case for Wiz to stay behind and join him in this venture. We have reached a crossroad and he is tempted. In the end he cannot forego the journey's end. He will return to Nashville. He leaves behind a CD and asks him to write. As they shake hands it seems to me they both know it will not happen. The magic is in the moment and the moment will pass with our departure.

Our thoughts are solemn and heavy as we drive down the interstate east toward Kansas City. No more than a few miles outside Boulder, Wiz suggests we turn back. The old hitchhiking ghost of Mustang, Nevada, returns to my mind. I had been more than prepared to stay another night but now it is too late. Don't turn back. You can never turn back.

Thoughts of what might have been will always linger but the moment is past. Should we return the experience could never live up to what we have already experienced. We have departed for a reason though we cannot fully understand what that reason may be. It is not our destiny. We came to the crossroad and made a choice. To turn back now would be to fly in the face of fate. Believe in the path and go forward.

Wiz concedes in retrospect. Had he insisted, I would have given him a ride back and left him to pursue his own journey. With the shadow of regret following, we drive on. Boulder has been all that we could have expected and so much more. We could have stayed. We both had reasons. We both made a choice. It is a place of magic, a place that called to us and spoke to our souls. I have no doubt that each of us will return.

If ever I am stranded on a lonely road alone

Here I will return to find a second home

If ever I am fallen like October leaves of brown
Here I will return to stand on sacred ground

For I will wander distant lands and glory at the sights
But I will never leave behind the wonders of this night

18

KANSAS HIGHWAY BLUES

We drive as long as our spirits will allow, finally pulling up at a trucker's all-night diner somewhere on the outskirts of a town called Limon. Wiz goes in and fills up with coffee and a bite to eat while I grab some needed sleep in Sally. My mind is swimming in a sweet and swirling torrent of dream. Esmeralda is with me. Though I have left temptation behind, her spirit follows me.
Is it real or is it the creation of my muse? Either way, is it wrong? Can a person betray his or her lover in dreams?
I have no heart to halt the passion that runs through my veins and fills my very soul with sweet, sweet delight. This is not my dream alone. It is too powerful. It is the dance of the temptress and gypsy magic. It is proof positive that we live our lives as spirit beings unconfined by physical space and time. It is far more than a sensual feast; it is a spiritual wonder. Our naked bodies blend and mold together, joined as one in magical rhythmic motion. Love among the stars, heaven's gate, defying eyes of the gods, the muse of heavenly poets, gardens of heavenly delight, the tender mercy of Eros, an endless dream of ecstasy in the liquid sanctuary of sensual fulfillment.

She dances by firelight in a gypsy caravan, bidding me with her hands and eyes to come. I follow as she lays her body down by a river of moonlit waters and opens to my embrace. She leads me to a forest of starlight and reveals her secret soul. She pulls me to her breasts, soft as down and charged with radiant pulsing force. She locks me in her hold. Our legs and arms enfolded, our bodies joined as one, we are capable of flight, no longer physical beings but pure embodied light. This is no dream. It is real. I have left this world behind.

Wiz emerges from the diner, renewed and ready to take the wheel. He senses my distance and allows me to remain in dreamland while he drives into the night. The land is flat and the road is straight and I am caught between worlds unable to shake the dream that has captured my soul. Onward we drive as I struggle to retain my hold on the earth. I am submerged in liquid, sinking ever deeper, aware but unafraid of drowning. I open my eyes and return to here and now, slowly regaining consciousness. Each time I go down it is harder to return, harder to pry my lids apart, harder to gain focus, harder to hang on to the waking world.

I let go. The dream takes hold of me. It is not mine to control. I will let it run its course. Let it take me where it will. I will fight no more. I will not struggle against the dream that embraces me. Let it be. Let it have its way with me. It is not for me to turn back my destiny though it beckons me to the edge. There are forces at work here that will not and cannot be denied. To do so would be perilous to my soul.

We reach the Kansas border in morning light. Wiz has lost his caffeine high and hands Sally's reins to me. The night's journey has provided sufficient rest to drive though I am not truly awake. I am entranced in a state of awareness. The world is transformed. A sky of endless clouds, huge white billowing formations roll over us, itself a dream within a dream. Never have I seen such a sky. It seems to cover all of Kansas, moving westward from the storms that have flooded the plains and valleys of the Missouri and Mississippi Rivers.

The dream takes on a new dimension. No longer confined to darkness, it summons me in broad daylight and dances in the corners of my mind. I need only call her name and she appears before me. As the miles roll on and the clouds begin to part, revealing scattered glimpses of blue sky above, I become aware of another presence in the dream world that still clings to my conscious being. It is my love, my gypsy queen a thousand miles away in Nashville. I glance in the rearview mirror and catch the startling sight of a whirling red light.

A Kansas highway patrolman pulls me over and informs me that I've been traveling at 73 miles per hour. The highway is desolate with little traffic and the speed limit is 65. I've been in another world unaware of his presence behind me. I suspect it is my lack of awareness and not the modest violation of the speed limit that has led him to pull me over. A sixty-five Mustang with California plates and a driver who has been on the road too long is suspect enough.

He asks for license and registration and I scramble to find them. In my haste I hand him the original registration. It is over ten years old. He walks back to his cruiser to check for warrants while I locate the current registration. When he returns I hand it over with my apology. He smiles and tells me he's going to let me off with a warning. He advises me to keep my focus on the road. It is a warning in more ways than one.

Wiz has awakened to this scene and realizes its nature before I do. "Sara just reached out from Nashville to give you a slap." I don't doubt it. We had lived apart for twenty years but always we were connected in spirit. I call for her forgiveness and feel it is received but forgiveness must be without judgment and it will be another thousand miles before the truth of what has happened here on an open Kansas highway will be revealed.

I have no guilt and will not be made to feel guilty. A man cannot control his dreams – certainly not a dream born of divine forces. I have not betrayed my love though I have forgotten for a time its source and fountain. I have discovered what I have always known within: that it is possible to love again. Love is always possible.

The closer we get to Nashville on the eastward swing of our journey, the more my thoughts will turn to her. I have loved her so long with so little reason. I knew from the first time I saw her in her layered gypsy dress, bandana wrapped around her wild wavy hair, brown with henna red, to keep from drifting over her almost childlike face, that she was the woman of my dreams. She was innocence and wisdom. Her eyes sparkled with anticipation of life's adventures. She was mystery and mysticism, reading palms and interpreting the stars. She was spirituality and sensuality with a voice that channeled angelic beings. An inspired dancer and musician, her talent shined like the sky of a million stars over Sonora Pass. She was unreachable, bonded to another man, mother of a small child, and I was neither ready nor able to vie for her hand. My love remained in my heart.

I would dream of her later when I tested the fates in New York. It was as if she called to me from across the continent and I answered with my devotion. When I returned to California, broke and struggling for a way forward, she was all I could think about. My roommate told her how I felt though I had not confided in him and my fate was sealed.

It happened one night in the back yard of a mutual acquaintance beneath the stars of heaven. We touched and I knew. I wonder how many of us are blessed to know such a feeling. To reveal the contents of the heart and know in an instant the meaning of love. All this and so much more than a thousand words could begin to describe in the mere act of touching.

We began a relationship of agony and ecstasy, passion and jealousy, joy and pain. Maybe it was too soon for the love of a life. Neither of us was prepared for such devotion. We were young and hungry for adventure. The world before us was too wide open and teeming with excitement to commit to another's dreams and ambitions.

It ended as suddenly as it began, in a fit of jealousy – not unfounded but unjustified. She had sworn her love but she had not forsworn her freedom. The final scene was darker than any I had known. For years I would refer to that event as the incubus. My betrayal, a jealous accusation, struck her so deeply that she threw herself at me in rage. When I realized what I had done I recoiled with remorse but it was too late. The damage had been done.

She called not long after to say goodbye. She was leaving the valley, bound for glory in Oregon. We parted as friends and for years I would follow her with a trail of love letters, hoping beyond hope to win back her love. Eighteen years later she would answer.

Her travels took her from Oregon to Idaho to Nashville in pursuit of her dream. Her daughter grew from a beautiful child to a mature young woman. She went through several frustrating relationships. She came to the realization that she was attracted to men who treated her poorly. They were broken spirits in need of nurturing and incapable of returning her love.

I had been through many changes. Broken relationships left me wondering about wasted time. I had managed to complete my Masters degree and found gainful employment in the public schools. My station was secure. I had a sacred circle of friends and a close family. I was alone but not lonely. I had decided not to settle for anything less than love. I believed and still believe that an individual can find happiness and meaning in life even if he or she never found that special loved one. I had the respect of my peers and I felt no animosity toward anyone in the world. I had arrived at a place of peace and contentment.

It was then that she came calling. I had seen her from time to time over the years so it was not unexpected. She'd made a habit of traveling and would drop by sometimes when her path came back home. We rekindled the flame on occasion but it was only that. I'd often feel empty when she departed.

The last time I saw her I drove her to Idaho to pick up some of the things she'd left behind. We left Modesto as lovers and arrived in Coeur d'Alene as friends. She made visits to former haunts and former lovers, leaving me to my own. She started speaking fondly of the man she left behind in Nashville. I had not realized until then that she still possessed the power to wound me. When we parted I made a vow that I would never welcome her into my life again.

I received her politely but guarded. Uncertain whether I wanted to see her but certain I did not want to resume any romantic involvement, I found her waiting on the steps of my front porch at two o'clock in the morning. She had wanted me to meet her at a bar and I had not responded. Something was different about her. Something had changed.

We talked through the night, rebuilt a bond and sealed it several evenings later. We made love as we had in the distant past when we were both young and eager to please. It was a union of spirits, a night to remember, and a twist of fate that would change the course of my life.

Whenever we are confronted with life altering choices, there are two questions we must ask and answer: First, do I want a change? Second, if so, how much do I want it?

The choice was clear. She wanted me to move to Nashville. Staying in California was never considered. She wanted me to support her dream and her career. Mine was an afterthought. I should have known and maybe I did.

We jumped the broom in Nashville at Christmas time and married in Tahoe the following April. Marriage provided her health insurance, an important consideration the older we get.

From that moment everything changed. The first year was a constant struggle, a battle of opposing wills. I had moved two thousand miles only to be virtually abandoned. We survived but the distance between us grew. We parted on good terms when I left on this journey but I had no idea who would greet me when I returned: the loving, caring wife or the incubus of opposition. I had invited her on this homeward journey. She made the choice to stay in Nashville. She said that I needed space and she was right. I had spoken to her only twice since I left and nothing much was said. I wanted to live in the moment, to leave my life and my problems behind, and that is what I had done.

We pull over at a Kansas visitors welcoming center, grab a complimentary cup of coffee and pick up a pamphlet on golf in the Jayhawk state. We select a course in Lawrence (near Topeka) that is billed as one of the best public courses in the state. The drive is long and lonely. Wiz sleeps and dreams drift in and out of my consciousness. It is as if I have yielded control of my conscious thoughts. The traditional golden sea of grain is overshadowed by a pervasive green born of the recent rains. Crows are everywhere.

We reach Lawrence, a college town, and locate the course with plenty of daylight for a full round. Laid out on rolling Kansas hills, the course is gorgeous with plush green grass, elevated tees, thick rough and evergreens lining the fairways. I step out of Sally and feel like I've stepped through a pressure cooker. Wiz says I look like five hundred miles of hard road. Thanks, I think. I feel worse. We check in at the clubhouse and sign up for nine. By the time we pull our clubs from Sally, we're due on the first tee.

I dub my drive and watch it dribble down the fairway, commenting to the starter that I'm just a bit road weary. He knows the feeling. He's a navy man and recalls the first round after a long stint at sea. The ground won't stop moving.

After a few holes I realize it's not going to get much better soon. Even worse, my spirit is down and on a downward trend. I haven't the heart for laughter and camaraderie despite the beauty of the course and the friendly nature of the folks we're paired with.

Wiz has engaged his teasing commentary, his attempts at humor, and it begins to wear on me. I am far gone and feeling helpless to recover. On the seventh tee Wiz tosses me a pink tee. It is a running joke between us. I refuse to use yellow and orange balls or yellow and pink tees. In my old school philosophy, balls should be white and tees should be anything but yellow (conjuring fear) and pink (indicating timidity). I know it's superstitious but golf is a game that honors superstition. The thing is: I'm wearing amber shades and can't tell the color of the tee.

This time it fails to draw a smile. I have no humor left in me, just a despondent shrug as I toss it aside. His reaction starts me rethinking the state of my being. With a downtrodden expression, he says: You hate me right now. I'm stunned. I had forgotten one of the important tenets of Zen golf: You are never alone on the course. Wiz has tried to lift me up and I have given him nothing but grief.

He nails a three-wood but it sails into the trees on the right. I step up and hit the best drive of my round dead center. When Wiz has trouble finding his ball I welcome the opportunity to make peace by helping him locate it. A load is lifted from my shoulders though my body remains bone tired. I finish well, hitting the last two greens in regulation.

As we walk off the ninth I realize our scores are

close. He in fact has bettered me by two strokes. The golf gods have spoken. Wiz is gracious in victory. I know he has waited for this moment though he would not say so. He offers excuses for my game but there are none. The gods have delivered a lesson in humility. For the second time the student has beaten the teacher in a fair test of golf. He refused to acknowledge his win at Tioga Pass and now he refuses to gloat. He could easily have stumbled and fallen short. The road has been as tough on him as it has on me. I'm proud of his accomplishment, proud of the way he carries it, and proud that he has overcome the poor attitude of his playing partner.

 I will contemplate this round for some time. I am not proud of my own behavior during the middle part of the round. Hanging my head, cursing myself, refusing attempts at encouragement, wallowing in self-pity. It is the kind of golf behavior I deplore in others and there is no excuse. Regardless of circumstance, there will be bad rounds. The game mandates it. There is a right way and a wrong way – or at least a better and worse way – to handle it. I chose poorly, seeking excuses and finding blame. The better choice would be to ask yourself what the round is teaching you. Had I asked that question I might have realized I was badly in need of grounding. I'd been swimming in a sea of dreams and could not get a grip on the earth. Sometimes you have to plant your feet and feel the pull of gravity. Next time I'll do better.

 We drive on to Kansas City, our thoughts dwelling on the game behind us. We need food and pull off at the first off ramp that looks inviting. The only choices that greet us are a pizza parlor and a Chinese restaurant with a karaoke stage. A rowdy man in front of the pizza parlor makes our choice for us. We walk into the Chinese restaurant and take a seat. We are the only customers in the place. The atmosphere should be peaceful but for an explosive telephone conversation in Chinese that the woman at the cash register is having. The waitress explains with a smile: "In laws."

Over tea and wanton soup I tell Wiz what I believe is the ultimate lesson of the round: Accept adversity.

On our way back to Sally we encounter another disturbance, a shouting match in the parking lot that looks like it might get physical. We decide that Kansas City is not our kind of town but we are too tired to move on. We stop at the first motel we come across where a man with a couple of teeth missing tells us: No Vacancy. We move on to a Motel 6 with the TV bolted to the wall and settle in for some deep sleep.

The first words that emerge as I awake are: Welcome adversity! It is not enough to accept adversity. In order to learn, one must embrace the experience. We learn more from adversity than we do from our best rounds. Wiz nods in agreement and we hit the highway once more, anxious to get out of this town. St. Louis here we come.

19

THE HEARTLAND

In the middle of Missouri, an approximate equal distance between Kansas City and St. Louis, lies the heartland city of Columbia. From the interstate the sight of a golf course draws us in for a round. For me it is a chance at redemption. For both of us it will be a landmark, a line in the sand we have chosen to honor: The sixth hole will be the 200th of our journey.

Wiz marked it as a goal after Grand Canyon – on the day we played three rounds on the road and drew the laughter of Don Juan. It required an average of about nine holes a day. We are not aware that this will be the last round of our journey but we are gratified to have reached this marker. Had we not reached it, it would not have mattered but, as it is, it is a cause for celebration.

It is a weekday and the course is far enough from town and the highway that we are virtually alone on the field of play. No one but a few devoted locals and us are on the putting green. I take care of the green fees while Wiz checks out a row of clubs against the clubhouse wall. He finds a Ping two-iron on sale for fifteen bucks and asks my advice. "Buy it," I tell him. The club is worth far more. It's in perfect condition and matches a Ping five-iron he found on a driving range, as if it was left there like the jazz shoes in Boulder for Wiz to find. Some golfers choose clubs; Wiz allows the club to choose him.

We later learn the club is brand new and likely put up for sale after its first round. The golfer who abandoned it may someday learn: It's not the club; it's the hands that grip it.

The man in the clubhouse takes us out to the first tee and gives us a verbal rundown on the course. He's as friendly as an autumn breeze. In all my days of golf I cannot remember ever receiving such personal and friendly treatment at any course at any price. It is a breath of fresh Missouri air and the course itself is a gem. An imaginative nine-hole layout, it features running water, deep forest, gullies, hills and dales, and tall trees of maple and oak with sprawling branches jutting at times well into the fairways.

We tee off and I'm immediately relieved. My game has returned to me. The gods of golf appreciate repentance. I par the first and hit a beautiful draw down the middle of the dogleg left second. Wiz bogeys the first and fades a well-struck ball off the second. It caroms down a 20-foot embankment. I take a look at his lie and offer: Looks like a two-iron to me.

It's a steep uphill shot that must carry a creek and a grandfather tree thirty feet high and just as wide. Wiz whips out his magic two and lets it rip, sending a masterpiece sailing overhead, clearing the creek, clearing the tree and settling just short of the elevated green. By my calculation the shot has covered a solid 220 yards. It is by far the finest shot he has hit in 196 holes. At an average of 5.5 shots per hole that's about 1,076 shots. Inspired by his moment of Zen, I spike a wedge to the stick and drill it home for birdie. Wiz chips up and makes par.

A high school kid, stocky and quiet, approaches us with an aura of intensity. We offer him a choice: Join us or play through. To my surprise he opts to join us. We play on, matching shot for shot, stroke for stroke, Wiz and I on a Zen golf high, the kid on his own intense ride. We try to loosen him up and lead him to the other side of golf. He is too much tension and technique but he has a feel for the game and a strong desire to master it. He has not yet learned to let the game master him. The game is the real teacher and it yields its secrets only to those who humbly give themselves up.

As we reach the landmark hole on the sixth tee the kid has earned the honor of hitting first. It is a long par four with a deep forest to the right. He pulls out his high tech driver with an oversized metal head and ultra-light graphite shaft, and nails one long and lean on the left side of the fairway.

"Nice shot," we offer.

He grins. It is as much emotion as his temperament allows. I pull out old reliable, Big Mama, my faithful persimmon driver, and summon the gods for the blessings of the journey. I give myself up, call on my inner being with heightened awareness of the fourth and sixth chakras, and let it go. She sails like a shooting star into the distant horizon, like a hawk catching an updraft, finding a second wind, rising and sailing again. Savor the moment, I tell myself. Savor the moment. We finish the round walking on air, breathing good tidings, taking in the smell of green, savoring the hillside surroundings wealthy in wildlife and plant life.

On the ninth tee the kid finally opens up and talks.

Throughout the round he has spoken no more than a dozen words. I tell him I hope to see him on the tour someday. He yields to another smile. It seems I've tapped his dream. "I hope so," he replies.

Having broken through, I ask him if he's a baseball fan. "Sure," he says. I get the feeling he's never met anyone who wasn't. "St. Louis or Kansas City?" He furrows his brow. This is a serious matter. "Well," he says, "I've always liked George Brett." He's a Kansas City man. "Sure fire hall of famer," says I. "Five years after he retires." I'm not sure, of course, but I think we've made the kid's day.

He struggles a bit on the ninth. He's not used to all this talk on a round of golf. But he keeps his cool and saves the hole. Maybe he will make the tour someday. Stranger things have happened. I hope so.

We finish up and the kid waits to replace the pin. We shake hands in the spirit of the game.

"Good luck," I offer.

"Happy golfing," says Wiz.

"Same to you," he replies.

He's off to the putting green. His day is not over. He will practice until the sun goes down. I wonder if he learned anything from these strange longhaired golfers who revere the game in a way he's never experienced or observed. I hope so. I know that we have learned from him.

They grow them strong in the heartland, sturdy and constant as the summer heat, quiet and grounded souls. We hang out a while, taking in the heartland glory, drink a beer and watch the locals walk slowly through their day. They never hurry.

There's a lesson here: Never hurry in the garden of Paradise. Take your time and savor the experience.

The lady at the desk watches the president on TV. We ask about the flood and she shrugs, "It's still there."

So it is. St. Louis and the great flood of 1993, here we come.

20

ST. LOUIS & THE GREAT FLOOD

Much has been said on this journey about the great flood of the northern Mississippi. For weeks now it's been front-page news. The latest reports surround the question: Will the floodwall protecting St. Louis hold up? The great rivers run higher now than they ever have in recorded history. Most of Illinois, Indiana and much of Missouri have been declared disaster areas. The bulging Mississippi and Missouri Rivers are cutting new channels in the earth and the map will forever be altered [6]. New streams, creeks and tributaries, new ponds, lakes and marshlands will be formed to change the land and rearrange its inhabitants.

It is a tumultuous event in the evolution of the planet but around here they don't talk about it much. What is there to say? You take it in stride because there aint much you can do about it. These are not the kind of people to panic and run. Other than the possible collapse of the floodwall, the big worry right now seems to be the drinking water. How ironic is that? With all this water fresh from the heavens, many communities have had to cut off the water supply. You just can't drink that river water. It's contaminated. I'm sure someone knows the answer to this equation but it seems to me a strange world when you can't drink the water. I first noticed it several years back in the Sierra Nevada. They had signs posted: Don't drink the water; it'll kill you. I believe it had something to do with deadly microbes. I don't know what the story is here. I suspect they've pumped so much industrial waste into the rivers it has to be filtered.

Driving through St. Louis on a bright summer day you'd never guess it was a disaster area. We have seen little evidence of the great flood from the vantage point of the interstate – only the immense rolling rivers themselves. Just north of St. Louis the Missouri joins the Mississippi from the west and the Illinois from the northeast, marking it as a critical flood zone. To the south the Ohio and Tennessee Rivers join forces at Paducah, Kentucky and feed into the Mississippi at Cairo, Illinois. The flood is confined to the north. By the time you get to Tennessee the worry is drought. The world is full of irony.

The Missouri crosses under the interstate at St. Charles on the outskirts of St. Louis. These are dirt water rivers, the color of creamed coffee. They look thick like porridge. Of the two, the Missouri is the more impressive to the eye. Its breadth is mammoth and you feel its powerful force even from the highway above.

A few scattered raindrops grace Sally's windshield, nothing more. There is a clarity of vision I have rarely seen in the heart of civilization, a brightness of colors, the sharp crisp angles of the skyline and the great St. Louis Arch. That it conjures an image of McDonalds is an inescapable fact of modern commercial life.

St. Louis strikes me as the first eastern city on Interstate 80, like Memphis on the southern route. The line is drawn at the Mississippi. It presents a sharp contrast to Kansas City, a town that seems to have neither western nor eastern roots, and an even greater contrast to Columbia. Its glory and its pain are wide open to the view of all who pass through its gates. Its stylish towers and skyscrapers, Victorian houses and classic neighborhoods stand in conflict to its multi-storied brick housing projects, crumbling buildings and concentrated poverty.

We see billboard advertisements of Gentleman's Clubs and Dancing Girls by the score. We take it as a sign. It's probably our last day on the road and the last major city we will encounter. We originally intended to catch a ball game here but our schedule is way off and the Cardinals are no longer in town.

We pick out an advertisement of a place that seems to be directly on our path. It's called *Cheeks* with an obvious reference to the female anatomy. We pull off the highway at the given exit and find ourselves in the middle of slum city. Welcome to East St. Louis. The only white people here are in the joint where we're headed. We drive about ten blocks when the red neon sign of danger lights up in my head. What could be more inviting to the criminal element than a couple of white boys in a bright orange Mustang with California plates?

I turn to Wiz and say, "Let's get out of here."

He's not ready to turn back.

"Let's give it a few more blocks."

A few more blocks and we pull into the parking lot of *Cheeks*. It's a flat top building with painted bricks and looks like it might have been a mechanic's garage in a former life.

Wiz ran out of cash somewhere between Boulder

and Kansas City. I hand him a twenty before we walk in and advise him not to sit in the front. It's not that I'm a veteran of these joints but I have on occasion admired the art of erotic dance. There's a world of difference between the "titty bar" where well rounded women with too much makeup shake their breasts, slap their asses and take your contributions in their bared "cheeks" and a true strip joint where the women move with the grace of cats or swans and stimulate erotic dreams with a blueprint of the male psyche.

This joint is somewhere in between. Inside it's nicer than its exterior would suggest with red carpeting, velvet drapes, a circular bar with padded barstools and several small stages lit in shades of red, blue and amber. We sit at the bar, order a couple of beers and turn our eyes to stage number one. The dancer is tall, thin, blonde and beautiful, a specimen worthy of her profession. If she's smart she'll give it up after a few years and have enough money to pursue the kind of life she chooses. Maybe it's just a dream but I choose to believe it can happen.

She dances with natural talent but her performance seems to lack imagination and choreography. It seems to me she's new at this. The song closes and Wiz hustles over to talk with the dancer. I'm not sure what he's up to and less sure that I like it. He returns with a shrug and an explanation: He wanted to buy me a table dance but the cost is twenty and after his beer he only has fifteen. I tell him it was not meant to be.

The next song starts up and she dances for me. She's certain she can get me to cough up the twenty and she wants me to know I'll get my money's worth. I resist the temptation but acknowledge her talent. There's a thin line between enjoying the erotic nature of the female form and blatant infidelity. It is a line I've chosen not to cross.

A man steps up to the dancer with a whisper and a bill and she springs into action. Wiz had it wrong. The specialty of the house is not the table dance but the lap dance. She straddles the man in an armless chair and grinds with a piston action that could turn back the floods. She presses her perfect breasts to his face and squeezes. She spins on a dime and continues her riveting motion with a backside view. All the while she maintains eye contact with us. She has marked us as the next recipients of her charms.

Suddenly she rises and stands like a statue before him. He produces another bill and she continues the ride. It reminds me of a mechanical bull or horse outside a supermarket. Pony up another quarter and let it ride. It is as close to sex as it gets without penetration.

Yes, I say to myself, this will do. Words begin to take form in my brain. It will be my first wet dream poem in a thousand miles. I signal Wiz, leave a five on the stage and we walk out into the startling daylight of a concrete maze. We stick to the plan: One beer and we're out of here. I'm a little surprised we live up to it.

Back on the interstate with Wiz at the wheel, the image of the dancer still fresh in our minds, words circle in my mind, finding their niche like pieces in a jigsaw puzzle. As we near the southern turnoff, I take out my notebook and write.

She was a streamline model nobody's whore
Breasts the size of golden delicious apples
She pressed her cheeks against the mirrored image
Of her own reflection and turned to squeeze

Her breasts together in a manner that suggested
Only one thing

Twenty bucks she said mouthing the words
Like licking a sweet round lollipop
Twenty bucks to feel the force of her machine
Finely tuned and oiled

Shake it baby grind it to the core
Squeeze it squirm and writhe
Drive it like a locomotive full of steam
Atomic powered submarine

Quake it take it break it down
Submerged in liquid lust
Glide the streams of wanton dreams
Buck and quiver like a wild stallion
Ride me high and bend me low
Take me to the poorhouse and drop me
Off the edge of sanity

Lay me down in tupelo honey
Leave me on the floating sea of fantasy

You've got to feed the monkey she said
Beyond the sweet blue flames of far away
The monkey has been fed

Fifteen bucks for a couple of beers and a wet dream poem. Not bad for a day's labor. She delivered on her unspoken promise. She gave me my money's worth.

[6] Having since read *Life on the Mississippi* by the

great Mark Twain, I now know this phenomenon has been going on a very long time. Human engineering will never be able to guide the great river where it does not want to go.

21

THE ROAD HOME TO NASHVILLE

    It has been a long and glorious adventure. Our minds and our souls have been fully consumed in the moment for the length of the journey. Only now do our thoughts return to Nashville. For the first time since somewhere in Utah we abandon the multi-lane interstate and settle into a rural American countryside. As we venture south on Highway 127 everything around us looks like Tennessee. The further south we travel, the denser the forest becomes.
    Here the night is serenaded by multitudes of clicking, screeching, croaking insects and tree frogs that are always heard but never seen. We glide through the rolling hills of southern Illinois, the bluegrass pastures of western Kentucky, the farms, dairies and grassland communities with their clusters of modern life, all night convenience stores, fast food restaurants and brightly lit gas stations. They almost seem out of place.
    This is the chosen land of the Shawnee, Natchez, Choctaw and Cherokee. It is the land of great rivers where thousands of Indian nations, faced with the onslaught of European invasion, condensed social evolution into a microcosm. The distinctive Indian burial mounds still mark the landscape. It is the land of pioneers as well, the Daniel Boones and Davy Crockets

who braved the dangers of the forest and moved on at the first sight of smoke on a distant hill. It is the land where the line was drawn for slavery and a great civil war. It is a land made rich with blood and sacrifice.

As we drive by the large, simply designed homes with their huge well-kept yards and open spaces between them, our minds drift to quiet times and simpler places to settle on the place we now call home.

This land holds special meaning for Wiz. He grew up in these parts. His grandparents still live here in a little town called Royalton. His old haunts are down the road in Pinckneyville. The place is filled with memories and Wiz grows quiet in remembering. This is his heritage: Small Town America.

Our first stop is Nashville, Illinois, population 3,202. We've talked about golf in Nashville and we decide to take advantage of an early opportunity. There are only a few hours of daylight left as we drive down the main street and turn at a small sign directing us to the local links. For a small town this version of Nashville features a wonderful park with lighted baseball fields, picnic tables, a driving range and a golf course all in one cozy package.

Driving down a tree lined, one lane road to the clubhouse, kids are playing ball to our left. I love baseball. Nothing brings out the kid in me more than a ball game. I tell Wiz I wouldn't mind watching a few innings but he seems anxious. We come to the clubhouse and Wiz lingers while I check out the scene. The door is locked and a circle of gray haired men, neatly dressed, is engaged in a heated discussion around a large wooden table behind a plexiglas wall. I think about knocking but something about it pushes me away.

I return to Sally and give Wiz an account of the scene and he decides to scope it himself. He comes back with the same reaction. There will be no golf today. It seems we've played our last round after all. It just wasn't meant to be.

We head out of town, feeling a bit let down, and reach Pinckneyville as the sun sets on the horizon to our right. It's a charming little town with forties architecture and a circular drive at its center. Wiz breathes it all in with a quiet air of nostalgia.

You can never go back, my friend.

I don't know if it's the contemplative scenery, Wiz's sentimental mood or thoughts of home but we pass on an opportunity to fill up with gas even though we are getting low. After a while I calculate the mileage in my mind and check out the road atlas. Sure enough, it looks like an adventure. The oversight costs us a planned detour to Royalton when the little town of Vergennes is closed for the night. I wonder if we put ourselves in this situation unconsciously: one more episode for the story, one more roadside anecdote, one more mystery to punctuate the tale. Can we make it or will we be stranded in the southern Illinois countryside camping by the side of the road?

I remember not so long ago discovering the key to mountain driving. Up to then the winding roads filled me with anxiety and feeling exhausted when I reached my destination. The secret lies in relaxing the solar plexus, freeing the third chakra of all physical tension. As if by magic the wheels bonded to the curve of the road and found its pace. When the inevitable maniac came sniffing my tailpipe I calmly pulled over to allow the hurried driver to pass. No panic. No tension.

I summon the technique now and it takes hold

almost immediately. There is an undeniable joy in taking risks, an attraction to the excitement and mystery of danger, real or imagined. I recall running curfew as a teenager, being chased by cops through back yards and alleys not knowing if a growling dog would greet you over the next fence and learning afterwards if your compadres managed to escape. It is a childish pleasure to be sure but it seems to me it's good to remember the child within from time to time.

We struggle into Carbondale, a veritable metropolis in these parts, and fill the gas tank at the first station. Sally's tank holds 17 gallons and we fill her with 16.3, close enough to justify the suspense.

We grab coffee and a burger at a fast food joint, wonder at how Carbondale resembles so many other towns across the country, toss over the idea of hitting a local bar and head out into the night.

We cross over the Ohio, Tennessee and Cumberland Rivers into western Kentucky just above Land Between the Lakes. We drive on in virtual silence, thoughts to ourselves, until a roadside attraction pulls us in one more time. Somewhere around Saratoga there is a late night driving range just off Highway 24 to Nashville. We refuse to pass it by.

There on a Kentucky roadside, two hundred and three holes and thousands of miles behind us, there in the land of a billion flying, crawling, buzzing and biting insects, I find the missing links that mold my golf swing into one flowing motion. A wider stance steadies my balance and playing the ball back toward center sends my long irons screaming into the darkness long and straight as a bullet. Here on the bug infested roadside I have found the Zen of golf. I know the lessons of this night may not apply tomorrow. The swing like the golfer is a dynamic and ever changing phenomenon. But for the moment the game and I are in perfect harmony. If all the lessons of golf can be reduced to one it is this: Savor the moment. Nothing in golf or in life lasts forever. When it all comes together, embrace it, cherish it, bask in it and create a vivid picture to remember it by.

It is unfortunate that two people so rarely experience the Zen moment at the same time. Wiz struggles with his swing and races through a large bucket of balls as if he is finishing a tedious task. By the time I'm down to twenty balls, he's done. The bugs are bugging him. He helps me finish up and we head out for the last stretch before Nashville.

The silence returns to us. When a sign announces, "Welcome to Tennessee!" I glance at my watch and say, "I've just turned forty." Wiz had forgotten. So had I for the most part until the last few hours. He wishes me a happy birthday and our thoughts return to home. Across the border "Exit One" takes on a whole new meaning. Someone said: Life begins at forty.

Somewhere overhead, hidden in darkness, a crow heralds our arrival.

22

THE JOURNEY'S END

We hit town between two and three o'clock in the morning. For the first time in a month I'm aware that it is the hour of the drunk driver. The Nashville bar scene is alive and well. It doesn't seem to matter what day of the week it is. Nashville operates on its own schedule. Its people are always out there, making plans, talking shop and dreaming up schemes until closing time.

We gas up Sally, give her a good pat on the dash for a job well done and cover the last miles of our journey. Wiz takes the back roads to his secluded house in Williamson County, twenty minutes from the heart of Nashville. His live-in girlfriend, a talented and spiritual woman who has been at various states of war with Wiz since I've been privileged to know them, is asleep. As he circles the house, trying to rouse her from dreamland, I wonder what kind of welcome he'll receive. They were not on the best of terms when we left. Then again, even when they were on good terms it was a rocky road. I've sometimes wondered why two people who find it so easy to get along in the world have so much trouble getting along with each other.

Both have strong wills. Both have healthy egos and an independent sense of identity, destiny and everything else that goes along with being human. I hope the soothsayers are right when they say: Absence makes the heart grow fonder.

Rhonda makes a brief appearance on the front porch, clothed in a robe and a pair of fluff slippers. With a smile and a hug she wishes me a happy birthday and welcomes us home. She offers no glimpse of the whirlwind that awaits me. We unpack in a matter of minutes and say so long. We'll talk tomorrow.

I don't know what I expected but it wasn't what I got. I had promised Sara that I would be back by this day. Given the volatile nature of our relationship, especially over the last year, maybe I had hoped that my birthday would set the tone of our reunion. But in the early hours of a still dark morning it made no difference. Momentous as it seemed, the celebration ended the minute I walked in the door.

Stumbling on the porch with a handful of belongings and fumbling for my keys, I'm surprised she doesn't come to greet me. I lower my things on the living room floor and look in on the bedroom. She raises her head and offers the kind of greeting you might expect after a night on the town.

"Hi, what time is it?"
"Late. How are you?"
She's not well – hung over and sick. She tells me she's built up her defenses by playing the "if" game.
"If he doesn't call today…"
"I did call."
"He doesn't care."
"I told you."
"If he doesn't call today…"

"I wanted to leave Nashville behind."
"I'll stop caring."
"I wanted to live in the moment."
"If he doesn't call today…"
"I needed time and space."
"He doesn't love me."

I explain and explain again but I know it doesn't matter. Nothing I say or do will make any difference at this point. She's determined to have this fight. She's prepared her thoughts to have it out.

Does she think I don't remember all the times I waited for her past two, four, six o'clock in the morning? Or how about those all nighters with some lame excuse? Does she really think I never questioned her love for me? Of course not. That's not what this is about. It's a power play. Either she wins and I'm in her debt or she loses and I leave. It doesn't really matter to her which way it turns. Either way she's protected. Either way she's the victim.

A part of me accepts blame for not calling and not wanting to call. A part of me believes this is karma for Esmeralda on the streets of Boulder. The better part of me refuses to accept blame. I will accept responsibility for what I have done or not done but I will not take on the burden of guilt. My anger rises to meet hers but I wonder what lies beneath this assault. The last time we talked she was in high spirits. What has happened to change that?

I summon the lessons of the journey but I am blocked. I feel like I've been blindsided.

I remind her gently that it is my birthday and we declare an uneasy truce. The gloom is as thick as the Missouri floodwaters. The journey is over. The nightmare has begun. It is a recurring nightmare and one that has haunted our relationship for twenty years. Born of jealousy and heartbreak, it erupts without warning and follows us like a shadow of death, coloring all it touches, leaving us devoid of hope and wandering aimlessly in the valley of doom. Love is not enough. Respect is not enough. It feeds on itself until it devours our bond. Even the angels seem to have abandoned us.

Sleep does not come easy but I hold onto it until well into the day. To my relief she has tempered her ill will. Her anger has abated and so has mine. We have moved into an uncomfortable place where we are civil on the surface yet beneath there lingers a foreboding wind. The conflict has not been resolved; it has only been pushed back another day.

The day passes with small talk and reserved conversation. I sketch out the journey and relate the mood of our California friends. She relates what little news she has of the happenings in Nashville. While Wiz and I have experienced a lifetime in the past four weeks, it seems Nashville has been frozen in time. Nothing has happened. Nothing has changed.

We make plans for a birthday dinner at one of our favorite Italian restaurants. I am hopeful. A little romance may rekindle flames from the ashes of our relationship.

We sit in the patio area outside and she tells the waitress it's my birthday. The waitress senses my discomfort and promises not to sing to my relief. The lighting is bright and there are several parties within view, dampening the spirit of romance. We order and continue small talk evolving around her conversations with her friends. They are all in agreement: My collection of Marilyn memorabilia must go.

She has a point. It all started with Humphrey Bogart and Charlie Chaplin and spread to cover the Beatles, Jimi Hendrix, Jim Morrison, Einstein, the Kennedy's, James Dean and Billie Holliday. The Marilyn thing got out of hand when my friends and family members latched onto it. Whenever a gift was called for, Marilyn was an easy solution. I finally had to ask them all to stop. The pleasure of collecting is more or less in discovery. There is little of the same gratification when others do the shopping.

I admit I was a little in love with the mystery of Marilyn and Norma Jean. I found in her some of the same qualities that attracted me to Sara. She possesses a mixture of innocence and experience, vulnerability and strength. Marilyn lamented the absence of a father figure and so did my wife. Her transformation from an orphaned child to the most appealing woman of her generation is one of the most intriguing stories of our times. I observed and honored her remembrance in much the same way I honored Bogie and Bacall.

My wife had decided that Marilyn was somehow at the heart of our problems. None of her friends approved and none would put up with it.

It did not sit well with me. I believe in heroes. I believe it is important to hold on to them. When a man abandons his heroes, he yields a part of himself. The abandonment of heroes contributes to a social malaise – a sense that life has no meaning and no glory.

I was being asked to sacrifice Marilyn on my fortieth birthday and I could not abide.

I ask her to stop, to move the conversation along, but she persists. It has taken on greater meaning to her. She is determined to have it out. I ask her again to let it rest but she ignores my request. In anger I tell her that my life in Nashville has been reduced to the confines of one small room and now she wants to tell me what I can and cannot have.

She walks out, leaving me with two platters of pasta and a bill. "Happy birthday," I say aloud.

I pay the bill and walk out in a Nashville night. She is nowhere to be found. I figure she's gone to one of the nearby bars to drown her sorrow. I decide to let her find her own way home. I go back to the house and sort through my options. Should I return to California? Should I go back to Boulder? Or should I spend another year in Nashville – maybe under a separate roof?

Within minutes of getting home and settling into my misery she calls. She has no money and needs a ride. My anger says to let her walk but I'm not that heartless. I hop in Sally and drive back to the scene of the crime. I locate her in the parking lot. She starts in where she left off. Now she is certain she was right. Before she only wondered, now she knows: Marilyn is my true love. She has always been my love.

Irony strikes me like of bolt of lightning. I'd faced this accusation in several relationships but the name was never Marilyn, it was always Sara.

Half way home I've had enough of this lunacy. To be accused of being in love with a dead movie star is more than I can take. I pull to the side of the road and ask her to get out. She relents just enough to get a ride home. She takes a vow of silence and holds to it. We arrive and I close the door to my room. It is over. I have no doubt. There is no love between us.

The journey is over. The nightmare is begun.

23

HOMELESS ANGEL

Who can say what form angels may take? On a late July morning in the shadow of the Parthenon in Centennial Park, he came in the form of a tough merchant marine down on his luck.

I get up and walk out early, determined not to encounter my wife and former love. I want no part of her and wish with all my heart I'd never set foot in this city. It felt like death. It's strange how I came to be in the park that day, my newspaper laid out on a picnic table, a large cup of coffee doubling as a paperweight to keep the news from blowing away. I had a habit of taking long walks on days like this when sorrow's shadow darkened my soul, but it was not my habit to hang out – unless to catch the bongo players and whirling rainbow dancers on summer Sundays.

I avoid contact with my fellow human beings. If a homeless man approaches I endure it for no more than a few minutes, give him a dollar or pocketful of change and be on my way. Not this time. This time a stranger walks up, looks me up and down, stopping and starting, measuring my receptivity before traversing the last few yards to my table.

"Mind if I sit here a spell?"

His voice has the bend of the deep south. He looks

haggard and I wonder if he spent the night here.

"It's a public park."

I'm hoping he'll make his plea, take a buck and go back to where he came from. I'm in no mood for a story but it looks like that's exactly what he has in mind.

"So it is," he replies as he plants himself across from me at the picnic table.

"Nice day," he says.

He wants to talk and he's not reading the signals that I don't.

He asks if I've seen a guy with a black felt cowboy hat with a golden Palomino embroidered on it.

"Not another like it in the world," he says.

"I haven't seen it but then again I haven't been here that long. You might want to ask the folks over there," I say nodding in their direction.

He doesn't take the hint. Maybe he's already asked them or maybe he knows them. He seems to know everyone in the park and they know him. Maybe this is his park and he wants to know what I'm doing in it.

He explains that someone stole his hat during the night. He doesn't know who but he refers to the thief or thieves as "them." He makes a point of saying he was drunk. It seems they stole a can of chili he was planning to eat for breakfast. He didn't mind the chili so much. If they'd asked he would have shared it with them. But that hat is another matter. It's a dirty low down deed to steal a man's hat. I agree with him.

He tells me how he's come to be living among the homeless in Nashville. He's on extended leave from his gig as a merchant marine. He calls it wild oats. He wanted to plant his feet on solid ground, get a feel for the country and mix with the common folk. Like Wiz he's an Alabama man. His check is overdue and he's out of money. He had it sent to a friend in Nashville but he's had trouble making the connection.

I can't help wondering what kind of friend would not offer his living room couch under these circumstances but I let it pass.

He says he once had a check sent general delivery to New Orleans but it took two weeks and that was two weeks too long. He doesn't trust the postal service and figures they stamp general delivery with their lowest priority.

Here in Nashville he's found himself in the middle of an ongoing controversy that has been on the front page of the Tennessean for weeks. The authorities want to ban the homeless from the parks altogether and clear the streets of them so that tourists don't feel threatened. Homelessness is bad for business. He tells me he's got a high-powered lawyer on the case and expects to meet with him later in the day. He figures the lawyer will want him to get arrested and he's willing to go along. I embrace his cause as noble and just. I wish him luck and figure they'll have their hands full if they tangle with this man.

His name is Reed and oddly enough I believe his story. Something about him lends him credibility. Except for the wrinkled look that comes from sleeping off a drunk in the park, his appearance is neat, his white shirt is clean, and his blue jeans are new. He wears an odd looking pair of high top tennis shoes. His black hair is greased and neatly combed. He has the look of a sailor, tough, slim and tightly packed. His nose is flat from too many bar fights. Put him in the ring and he could have been a contender for the welterweight crown.

After every story or commentary, told with the rigor and excitement of a carnival barker or a big tent evangelist, he checks in with the same remark: *I don't mean to be preaching and I know you don't need to hear this but then again maybe you do.* He looks me dead in the eyes and I perceive that he believes my sincerity just as I believe his.

Yes, my friend, I do need to hear this. We all need to hear it as often as it takes to shake us from our lethargy. It can't happen to me. But it can. It can happen to any of us. If we close our eyes to the root problems, ship the homeless out of town under cover of night, pass an ordinance banning them from the parks and the streets, then somehow the problem will cease to exist. The fact is: There ought to be jobs for anyone who wants to work. As long as there are not, the parks should be open to everyone everywhere, a refuge and a sanctuary. Tents and shelter should be put up along with free food, health care and decent clothing. Arts and crafts should be taught until the parks become a home and a source of pride to the nation.

He picks up my curiosity regarding his high tops and tells me his philosophy about helping a man in need. "There's always someone more needy than you are." He tells me about an old man who could hardly walk because his shoes were two sizes too small. Reed had a new pair of Nikes, solid walking shoes, and gave them to the old man. The man thanked him two or three times and shared his wine. A man who witnessed the transaction gave him the shoes he's wearing now. "That's how it should be. People helping people."

He pauses, catching his breath and gathering his thoughts. Then he speaks the words I was meant to hear: "Yeah, I'm down now. I'm a drinking man, a workingman, too, but a drinking man, and I like to fight and cuss. But I know one thing: *God don't give us no trials we can't bear.* As long as I keep my head up, I know I'll be alright."

I let it sink in for a few moments before I respond: "Brother, you are a preaching man, too, and the best I've ever been blessed to hear." Like the old man with the Nikes, I thank him two or three times and tell him I've got to go. "There's something I've got to do." I pull out a twenty and hand it to him. "I know it doesn't make any difference but there it is. It belongs to the world. Use it any way you like."

He takes it with a smile and makes a point that he never asked for it. He tells me one more story about going to church on Sunday where they blocked him at the door and told him he wasn't properly dressed. He blew fire and brimstone at their self-righteous faces. He quoted line and verse until they changed their minds. He changed his mind as well. "I can see this ain't a house of God after all."

With that we parted. I walked back home, clinging to the words that changed my water into wine. I hoped it would have the same effect on my wife.

I walk in to find her in the same cold and bitter mood with which I had awakened that morning. I want desperately to speak the words that the homeless angel had given me but I can't speak them to a face so cold. I stand still and watch a change come over her. She softens and asks, "Is there something you wanted to say?"

Yes, I respond, and speak: "God doesn't give us any trials we can't bear."

She waits, gazing into my eyes, and suddenly flies

into my arms. Love is reborn.
Thank you, preacher man, and thank you again.

24

THE JOURNEY CONTINUES

After a few days of peaceful rest, we take to the road with a plan to revisit a place Sara has discovered in my absence. Like Ponce de Leon she sought the magical waters of enchantment and youth. She found them at Hot Springs, North Carolina. Nestled in the Smokey Mountains among white bark birch trees and deciduous forest, it is accessible only to those who know its secret. As we drive in we observe a mining operation that reminds us nothing lasts forever. This forest is marked for clearing and when that happens everything will change.

We set up camp in a tent at the side of a creek by daylight and walk down a trail to the hot springs at night. There, in a world of torchlight and canopies, we are as removed from the reaches of civilization as we would be on the moon. A storm is brewing as we are escorted to our private spa. The moment is magical. I cannot imagine a more enchanted place for renewing the bonds of love.

From the deep bowels of the earth spring waters of heaven. The sight of my love's silken skin, the joy of her touch, the shine in her eyes under blue moonlight, combine with nature's splendor to form a feeling of well being so profound that death itself could not disturb this peace. Even a crack of thunder in the distance from the closing storm cannot break the spell. The collapse of a nearby tree limb under the force of the wind only heightens my sense of wonder.

Sara holds on to reason and rouses me to dress just before our escort comes to guide us in. Lightning fried customers are not in the business plan. They promise to give us an allotment tomorrow to complete our time in heaven. I am reminded of Grand Canyon and the pull of the ledge. Any longer in paradise and I might not have returned.

We use our allotment the next morning as we prepare for a drive to the coast. We plan to meet a friend at Myrtle Beach, South Carolina. He is hoping to find a new life. After that we will head north or south as the spirits move us, in search of an ocean view.

Myrtle Beach is a golfer's paradise. How strange is that? It has stores devoted entirely to golf balls. They tell me there are at least twenty courses here, ranging from championship layouts and country clubs to a public course for the common man. The streets are crowded with tourists and the beach itself has been cut down to a thin line by encroaching summer homes and oceanside resorts.

We find our view down the coast at the Barnacle Inn in Garden City. I serenade my love with newfound inspiration on a borrowed trumpet and we make sweet music before and after a moonlight walk on the sands of the Carolina coast.

There is no place I'd rather be
Than here beneath a moonlit sky
Counting endless waves of time
Arm in arm heart to heart

Her love embracing mine

We gather seashells and ocean carved rocks and allow the waves to carry us to faraway places, where we recline on sheets of satin in deep caverns at the top of crystal mountains. Sara wants to make an offering to the sea as a token of our love and gratitude. At the moment she stoops to gather in a stone with curious markings, a jewel she has long treasured slips from her necklace and is swept away. We search for it before deciding it was meant to be. She has made her offering. She will wear the stone she has just found in its place.

We arise the next morning at dawn, walk down to the beach, and hit five-irons into the Atlantic. This is my offering to the sea. Good people of all makes and sizes walk by with smiles, seagulls soar overhead, tracing the shoreline, and my mind drifts to a thousand places at once: Grand Canyon and the eyes of a crow, Albuquerque and a poetry café, Graeagle and a family reunion, Modesto and a sacred circle of friends, Berkeley and a modern poetry sage, Pacific Grove and golf in the kingdom, Yosemite and Tioga Pass, a sky of a million stars, Boulder and a mystical dancer, Kansas and a round of adversity, the St. Louis floods and Nashville's homeless angel.

This journey has no end, not for those who live each day, each hour, each moment as if it is the only moment of their lives. Not for those who embrace life in all its wonders, seeming good and bad, its glories and its trials. Maybe the most fundamental lesson of all is this: All our trials are for a reason. They instruct us by leaps and bounds to understand what might otherwise take a century. Life is too short not to embrace all of its experience. We are no stronger than our adversaries, real or imagined. Like Native Americans and warriors of old, we should honor our enemies and embrace the challenges that fall on our path. They make us worthy and strengthen our spirits. As long as we keep moving forward, keep listening, keep learning and remain open to the lessons of our never ending journey, we will not only survive but thrive.

On the road back to Nashville we stop to make camp at Altoona Reservoir in the Red Top Mountain National Park. We plan a good night's rest but end up staying two nights and the better part of two days.

Sara busies herself with a thousand projects, playing guitar, writing songs, making dolls from found materials, improving the campsite and communing with nature while I spend most of my time studying the rocks in their rich variety of petrified wood, crystal, stones of red, white and ash. On the second day, as I wash and examine rocks by the Creekside, there is a great commotion in the sky. At least a dozen crows gather in the trees overhead. I make eye contact with the leader. He tells me I have found it. Nothing more or less. With a great caw he takes flight and the murder of crows is gone.

All is well. All is as it should be. There is no journey greater than this we are on and always will be. There is no end and no beginning greater than love.

25

POST SCRIPT

The last I saw of Wiz he had joined forces with a master artisan known as Whittler. They were throwing an informal dinner party to commemorate the completion of a project, a blue moon recording of Wiz on a variety of flutes, from bamboo and wood to his magical silver masterwork, and Whittler on a variety of wooden percussion instruments carved from the forest around him. They call it: Cave Man Physics. The Wiz and the Whittler seems a natural name for their union but they choose to call themselves: The Hermetic Henchmen.

Rhonda is away, seeking peace and solace on her own journey at her farmhouse in upstate New York. Her relationship with Wiz continues its wild ride of on again, off again, in waves of agony and ecstasy. Like George and Martha of Virginia Woolf fame, maybe that's how they want it despite themselves. In any case it is the way of karma and the way it is. I pray they learn the required lessons and move on.

Wiz and Whittler are taking their show on the road to Atlanta, armed with a hundred recordings in leather pouches and a large leather bag of small, carved wood heads with open mouths. They call them whistlers. They're sure they will be a hit with the fringe art crowd in Atlanta. So it is written. They are artists on the cutting edge and are determined not to profit by their work. So be it.

Life in Nashville goes on as if nothing has happened since the great war. Cicada sing their nightly laments to the faded glory of the South. Songwriters scan the nightlife with furrowed brows, training their ears for the hook that will put them over the top. Vanderbilt students come and go, secure that the world revolves around their latest sporting event. The Grand Old Opry buys a little more of downtown in the name of manifest destiny.

Amidst it all, Sara and I dream of traveling to faraway places, oceanside vistas with natural graces, and rejoice in the blessings of the moment. We have for now survived the darkest hour. We will again do battle with the demons and ghosts that shadow us. We know that relationships have their trials. We are certain we will never again doubt our love. We will remember the lesson of the homeless angel and realize that all our troubles are for a reason [7]. We will overcome.

I have heard little from my California friends and loved ones. Time is filled with the living of life. We have our own lives, our own dreams and our own journeys to engage.   But in quiet times, gathered around fires, listening to music, enjoying a round of golf or searching for signs in the stars, I will think of them and the long stretch of highway we once shared.

[7] The relationship lasted four more tumultuous years. God may give us no trials we can't bear but there comes a time when the marriage is itself a barrier to growth. I returned home to California.

APPENDIX ONE

ZEN GOLF TOUR

June 30: University of New Mexico, North Course, Albuquerque NM, First Round

June 30: Puerto del Sol, Albuquerque, Low-Flying Aircraft

July 1: University of New Mexico, Beginners Course, Zen Golf Lesson

July 2: Glen Canyon Country Club, Page AZ, Woman Bartender

July 2: Coral Cliffs Golf Course, Kanab UT, Wind Blown Red Rocks

July 2: Thunderbird Golf Course, Mt. Carmel Junction UT, Don Juan Laughs

July 4: University of Pacific Feather River Inn, Graeagle CA, Family Reunion

July 5: Ponderosa Golf Course, Truckee CA, Traffic Jam

July 9: Pacific Grove Municipal, Monterey CA, Golf in the Kingdom

July 10: Modesto Municipal, Modesto CA, Wiz's First Birdie

July 11: Dryden Park, Modesto, Hot Shot Companion

July 12: Manteca Park, Manteca CA, Jere and Patty

July 13: Creekside, Modesto, Robert, Sue & the Ghost of Sam Snead

July 14: Wawona, Yosemite National Park, Rattlesnake without Rattles

July 16: White Pine Golf & Tennis, Ely NV, Welcome Golfers!

July 18: Alvamar, Jayhawk Nine, Lawrence KS, Round of Adversity

July 19: Kemper Golf Club, Boonville MO, 200 Holes

Total: Seventeen rounds, 203 holes, in 20 days.

APPENDIX TWO

SALLY'S MILEAGE

Nashville TN: 42,047 miles, 3.6 gallons
Memphis TN: 42,279, 11.6
Little Rock AK: 42,446, 9.2
Okemah OK: 42, 675, 10.8
Clinton OK: 42,881, 11.3
Amarillo TX: 43,098, 11.8
Cuervo NM: 43,271, 8.7
Albuquerque NM: 43,500, 12.5
Gallup NM: 43,659, 8.3
Tuba City AZ: 43,862, 11.0
Page AZ: 44,091, 11.5
Zion UT: 44,202, 5.6
Beaver UT: 44,312, 6.8
Ely NV: 44,500, 11.5
Fallon NV: 44,808, 13.1
Graeagle CA: 45,061, 13.1
Turlock CA: 45,394, 15.0
Modesto CA: 45,423, 3.5
Santa Cruz CA: 45,640, 12.2
Los Banos CA: 45,820, 8.9
Modesto CA: 46,008, 11.5
Wawona CA: 46,149, 7.9
Yosemite Village CA: 46,267, 7.1

Bridgeport CA: 46,444, 10.2
Tonopah NV: 46,624, 4.4
Ely NV: 46,821, 10.4
Hinckley UT: 46,999, 10.5
Salina UT: 47,086, 4.4
Crescent Junction UT: 47,238, 9.4
Glenwood Springs CO: 47,449, 12.9
Boulder CO: 47,639, 10.0
Limon CO: 47,795, 7.0
Hayes KS: 48,062, 13.7
Topeka KS: 48,317, 12.2
Columbia MO: 48,547, 13.0
Carbondale IL: 48,820, 16.3
Nashville TN: 48,070, 13.6

Total Mileage: 6,013 miles

The Handbook of Zen Golf

EDITOR'S NOTE

This is an abridged version of the original work. Its original intent was to be used as a guide to *The Pocketbook of Zen Golf*. The Pocketbook was to be used as an oracle. What survives here are eighteen lessons for a round of golf.

Its original authors were the fictional characters Shivas MacDuff and Rufus McGhee, the chosen alter egos of the main characters in *The Grand Canyon Zen Golf Tour*. From the original back cover:

Like the *I Ching* and *Tarot* to philosophy, *The Handbook of Zen Golf* is the oracle for those who love the game and seek to enhance their time on the course. Guaranteed to improve the round, it is likely to improve your game as well. Ranging from the practical to the esoteric, the handbook offers eighteen lessons that correspond to 108 messages from the collective pocketbooks. By revealing the lesson or lessons of the round, it opens the door to a new perspective of the greatest game on earth.

The Handbook of Zen Golf

A Reference Guide to
The Pocketbook of Zen Golf

by
Shivas McDuff & Rufus McGhee

INTRODUCTION

Golf is a spiritual game, a mystical game, a game that defies analysis and synthesis though dozens of magazines, countless books and recordings devote themselves to that cause. It is an endless pursuit because there is no ultimate solution. It is a game that is infinitely greater than the sum of its parts. And yet it is a simple game: the striking of a round ball to a chosen target. It is as simple and complex, illusive and accessible as the concept of Zen. Both embrace the spiritual, acknowledge the mystical and engage their followers in a lifetime of seeking.

The creators of this work consulted a serious student of Zen for his opinion. While he embraced the concept he said: It's sound advice but is it Zen? Without belaboring the point it occurred to us that we were using Zen in a more generic way: To connote the spiritual, mystical, existential and transcendental qualities of the game.

What is Zen? It seems to me the best answer is: Yes. To limit the concept of Zen Golf would not be Zen. Simply stated, Zen is, Golf is and Zen Golf is what you make of it. The only rule is there are no rules. Zen be with you.

Without Balance there is Nothing

*Stand with your posture
Balanced like a scale
Your movements should revolve
As the turning of a wheel*

*Wong Chung Yua
Circa 1600*

LESSON ONE

Balance is the First Lesson

It is difficult to imagine anything in life or in golf more important than balance. The force that is needed to propel a stationary ball 200-250-300 yards from a fixed position to a given target is astonishing. I have seen that force raise a large man off his feet and set him firmly upon the earth. I have seen it hurl the striker in a full sprint at a ninety-degree angle from the flight of the ball.

With such tremendous forces at work in the swing of a golf club, each possessing the inert power to send the shot awry in any direction, it is imperative to remain planted and centered in the position of addressing the ball. Locate your center and the field of balance surrounding it. Sense the circular boundary, acknowledging that you can lose your balance on the forward-backward plane as easily as the left-to-right plane. The coil of the swing must remain within the field of balance, focused at the core, even while shifting weight, throughout the course of the swing. Find your optimal stance and stay within yourself.

Without balance there are no other lessons. With balance all things are possible. As a wise person once said: When life is in balance, the soul is lightened.

LESSON TWO

Smooth and Easy Takes you Home

In the immortal words of the great Julius Boros: Swing easy, hit hard. Anyone who ever saw the master play knows the meaning of poetry in motion. Grip the club firmly but gently, give it a playful toggle, step to the ball and let it fly. It requires no strength, no great effort and no mental torture. It only takes a smooth, natural, easy flowing motion, a sense of rhythm and grace, and a feel for the sweet spot.

Let everything else go. Think of Boros and Casper. Think of a flowing river or stream. Picture the waves of a calm Pacific Ocean or sailing off a tropical island. See the flight of the condor. Consider ballet or the running motion of Willie Mays circling under a fly ball. Think of blue velvet and the voice of Lady Day. Think of a Carlos Santana guitar riff and let it flow. See yourself on a starlit flight, no cares and no worries.

Swing easy and let the pendulum sway of the club head locate the sweet spot on the white round sphere below. Be patient. It will happen. Golf is a game of opposites: Swing easy, hit hard.

The Shot

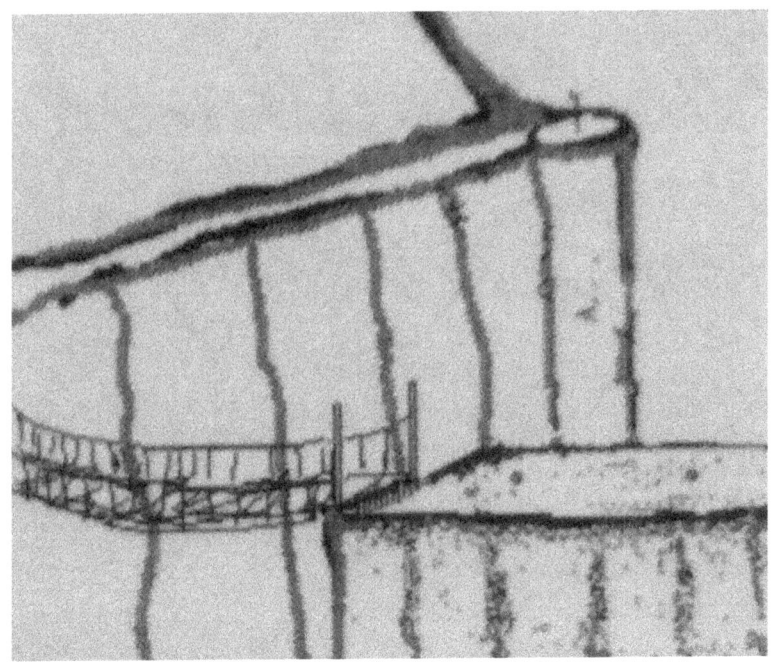

*Sit for a hundred years and then
Sit for a hundred more*

LESSON THREE

See the Aura; Visualize the Shot

Everything is energy. Everything is life. Everything is surrounded by fields of light and shadow, color and sound, waves of pulsating, breathing life force. Kirlian photography has recorded the aura surrounding all living things, observed by mystics and psychics since the beginning of time. Audio recording techniques have documented the storage capacity of trees and stones. The hills have eyes and memories and minds.

See the ball in a new light. Use your peripheral vision. Use your third eye. Focus from your inner vision until you see the aura surrounding the ball. Sense its pulse, its vibrant energy, its self-generating force. See the aura of the club head, the shaft, your hands, arms, legs and body. See the trace remaining in the path of the swing. See the fields of light become one with the ball, the swing, the club and you. See the trace of the ball in flight. Visualize the aura of the ball uniting with the aura of the club, enveloping the golfer, bringing together the motion of the swing with the flight of the ball.

Look around. See the fairway before you as fields of energy in shades of light and color. See the aura of the wind, the trees, the sand, the water, the rough, the grass, the earth and the heavens. Become one with all.

LESSON FOUR

It has nothing to do with the Score

Golf is a sacred game. It is a game that can bring you closer to the heavens and closer to the earth. It can bring you in touch with forces infinitely greater than yourself. It can give you a sense of profound peace, exhilaration, joy and love of life.

To those of us who truly love the game, though we may possess no more than a particle of understanding, it has nothing to do with the score.

I have seen a golfer hit the drive of his life only to break down in misery over a missed putt. I have seen grown men transformed into nursery school children because of a number placed on a scorecard. I have seen otherwise honorable persons pretend they cannot count to seven. To these people we have one suggestion: Bowling. You may be content with your game but the game – as well as those forced to play with you – will be better off without you.

What would you rather do? Play good golf or score well? The Zen golfer has no conflict. Play the game and let the score take care of itself.

*Pacific Grove
California*

Golf in The Kingdom

LESSON FIVE

Take Time to Enjoy the View

It is not a coincidence that the game of golf is played in some of the world's most beautiful natural settings. An ocean side links course can inspire absolute awe. A mountain course in a pine forest can elevate the spirit. Even the flatland and desert courses possess a beauty and charm to those who are in tune.

No matter where you tee up on your next round, take time to enjoy the view. There are few things more disturbing than the golfer who is so absorbed in his game that he would fail to notice the northern lights or a tornado on the horizon. Yet the incidental clearing of a throat or the landing of a butterfly will distract the same golfer during his backswing.

Find the beauty. Acknowledge the blessing: Another day in Paradise. Observe the trees be they pine, maple or oak. Become aware of all colors, shades of blue, green, red, brown and gray. Notice the presence of wildflowers, the scent of sage, wild grass and shrubs. Acknowledge the birds and wildlife that inhabit these sacred grounds. Enjoy the view from every angle. Become a part of it. See yourself as the center of wonder. Become one with all. It will then become impossible not to enjoy the round.

LESSON SIX

Find the Center

The golf swing is like a spinning top. When balanced and centered, it unfolds in fluid motion. It is a marvel, a marriage of force and counter force, motion and stability. Lose hold of the center – even by a fraction – and the swing wobbles, stumbles and falls.

> *When in stillness be as the mountain*
> *When in motion be as the river*
> Wu Yu-hsiang, 1812-1880

Centering is more than balance. It is grounding and mental focus. It is feeling the earth and the power of gravity below your feet. It is blending with that force in perfect harmony. Begin with balance and finish with grace. As you take your stance imagine a line, like a string or a rod, from the heavens to the core of the earth. Imagine it courses through your spine. Forget about ball striking. Forget about the grip. Forget about left-arm-straight and keep-your-head-down. Focus all energy on centering the swing on it axis from the backswing coil to the follow through. The centered golfer is consistent. The centered being is on the path to awareness.

LESSON SEVEN

Trust your Creative Impulse

No two shots are alike. Like wildflowers on an open field, they may look alike but they vary in texture, color, shape and posture. Each has its own distinctive being though its essence is shared. It is one of the blessings of golf that its variables are infinite. Play the shot as if it is the only chance you will ever have to make it – for in fact it is.

When you understand this you will begin to allow your imagination free reign. You will see possibilities that did not before exist. You will have greater appreciation for the challenge of the moment. You will not think back to the previous shot. You will not think ahead to the next. You will observe the peculiarities of the lie, subtle shifts in the wind, the bend of the trees and the contour of the fairway. The shot awaits and beckons your creative powers. Answer the call.

It is unfortunate that modern golf technology has so limited the variables of the shot. The controlled fade, the slice, the hook and the draw, the high and low flight of the ball: they are as much of the game as the straight shot. The greatest players the game has known have always bent the ball to their will. Trust your creative instinct. Free your mind and play the shot.

LESSON EIGHT

Feel the All Force

You can't see it but you know it's there. You can't hear, touch or smell it but its existence is beyond doubt. You can feel it in your soul. It is the wellspring of all power and energy. It is accessible to those who know how to summon it to their cause.

The all force exists deep within the soul of self. It is the universal self, the self that denies the self. Some can find it through meditation, music, dance, yoga, Tai Chi or any other means of achieving higher or altered states of consciousness. Once found it can be found again. The force is always within you though it must be summoned.

Begin by clearing your mind. Focus your awareness on the center of your being. Some say it is the solar plexus, the gut or the third chakra – an area between the naval and the breastbone. Some say it is the area of the heart or the fourth chakra. Still others say it is between the two or the area of the diaphragm.

The Zen Golfer must locate his or her own center and learn to summon it. It is the spring of the force within. Let it guide your swing.

LESSON NINE

Pay Attention to the Signs

By the third tee at Wawona Golf Course in Yosemite National Park there is a sign: Beware of Rattlesnake without Rattles. Some signs are easier to read than others. One does not look for golf balls in the rough of Wawona's third hole.

Most signs are more difficult to read. The Zen Golfer must be open and aware. When a sign appears it is up to you to interpret and heed it. Signs may come from many sources: a crow sounding a woeful caw, a ray of sunlight through the shadows of tall trees, a burst of chill wind or a sudden calm. Signs may be interpreted as warnings or blessings. In golf as in life there are times for caution and times for running with the wind. Your approach to the round at any given moment should be determined not only by awareness of the inner self but by an equal awareness of the environment. You are never alone on the golf course – even when playing solo. With practice and careful attention you can benefit greatly by listening and observing what the world has to tell you.

Signs are everywhere. They may mean different things to different people. Be aware, interpret them and learn from inevitable errors.

LESSON TEN

Pure Thoughts yield Good Shots

So you like to play mind games? You've come to the right place. Golf is a game of the mind. It is in fact possible to play a round of golf sans club, sans ball, sans everything, within the fertile confines of the ever-expanding mind.

Can you bend the path of a ball with you brain? Can you send it soaring like a rising seagull with a thought? Everyone who has ever played the game, from the master to the unskilled hacker, knows well the dark power of the mind. A negative thought is the surest way to destroy a golf swing. "Watch out for the trap on the right" sends the ball like a magnet straight to the sand. Pulling out a flawed ball for a shot over the water multiplies the probability of a one-shot penalty. The mind betrays – or rather we betray the mind.

The masters know the positive power of the mind. Believe it and it is done. Know that you can make the shot and allow the body to deliver it. Brain the ball. Talk to it. See it in the mind's eye. The mind holds the power. Free it of all distractions and watch with utter amazement the miracles it can deliver.

LESSON ELEVEN

Relaxation is Key

What is the worst thing that can happen? Relax, breathe deep and place yourself in a cool breeze state of mind. Smile. Nothing destroys the tempo, balance and rhythm of the swing more assuredly than tension.
Where does tension find its home in your physical being? For some it centers in the shoulders. For others it may be the lower back or the solar plexus. Locate the centers of tension in your body. Close your eyes and imagine the waves of a calm Pacific or a scenic lake. Use that image to create waves of relaxation and send them, wave after wave, throughout your physical being, focusing on the centers of tension. Think of nothing else.
When you have achieved a state of calm relaxation, begin the swing. Swing slowly, smoothly, careful not to disturb your relaxed state of mind and body. Practice your relaxation technique on each and every shot – even your putts. Become aware of tension when it appears, locate and dissolve it.
Allow nothing to come between you and your calm – not the score, not the taunting of fellow players, not an event of perceived misfortune. You are the master of your state of being. Don't panic. Remain calm. Breathe and relax.

LESSON TWELVE

The Infinite Round

Henry Miller said: Sit still and watch the world go round. The Buddha presented the lotus. How do we describe the essence, the life within the life, the core or the Zen? We must first recognize that it is not the Zen; we must then recognize that it is.

Contemplate the white of the ball. It is not a color. It is the presence of all light. It is the red road of the Cherokee, the white buffalo of the Lakota and the sacred white wolf. It is the moon in full, illumination, enlightenment and purity of spirit. Consider the infinite round. It is the great seven-spoke wheel of life, the wheel of dharma, the life-death-rebirth cycle, the four seasons and the endless motion of formation and transformation. Consider the meaning of the hole: It is the void, the unknown, the dark forest and the great mystery.

The white of the ball, the infinite round, the number nine and the path of a fairway: Such sacred symbolism is not a coincidence. We can only scratch the surface.

Golf is everything. Golf is nothing. Golf is life. Golf is not important. Contemplate a hundred years and think again. Consider the Upanishad: Those who understand do not understand.

LESSON THIRTEEN

Praise the Gods

The gods of golf are watching. Always. They know your thoughts and the content of your heart. The gods can be harsh and cold to the unworthy. They are kind and forgiving to the humble. The gods appreciate the player who expresses gratitude and the player who embodies grace. The gods shine on the golfers who are aware of those around them. The gods appreciate good manners.

The gods are the keepers of golfer karma. They punish golfers who habitually complain and curse and fail to offer thanks. They punish those who engage in petty gamesmanship, golfers who cheat and golfers who wish their playing partners ill fortune. The gods of golf hold the scale upon which karma is weighed. They control the flow of yin and yang. They giveth and they taketh away.

Take note when fortune appears to have turned its back. It is a test of your character. Know that in the absence of anger, good fortune will return. Remember that it is easy to be calm and collected when all is well; it is difficulty to maintain that balance when all is not well. When the gods frown, be humble and learn. When the gods smile, be humble and give thanks.

LESSON FOURTEEN

Every Round has its Lesson

The game is as complex as life itself. It is the chess of sport. No single source could ever attempt to cover all possibilities. The lessons of the round are as varied as the game.

As you play your next round, ask yourself: What is this round teaching me? The first answer may be balance – as it so often is. As the holes unwind, however, you may begin to recognize the singularity of the round. It is rarely as simple as balance. It may take hours or days to realize the lesson. It is always related to the player's life outside the game. The lesson may be humility for golf is ultimately a humbling game. Are you too focused on yourself to the neglect of your surroundings and those who share the view? The lesson may be pleasure. Are you taking your job too seriously? It may be a question of values. Can you see the forest for the trees? The possibilities are endless but you can be sure that whatever happens in life will reveal itself in a round of golf.

A Zen Golfer playing a miserable round was convinced that the cause was fatigue. He awoke the next morning with the thought: Embrace adversity. The round was preparing him for events to come.

LESSON FIFTEEN

Welcome Adversity

Take a moment to recall your most memorable shots: the low fading riser out of the rough, through the trees, below the overhanging branches, bending with the fairway, soaring like a hawk, landing like a butterfly safely on the green. Remember that bank shot through the sand or the blind draw over the valley of death to an elevated green. These are the moments inspired by adversity. It is the challenge that so often triggers the creative instinct.

The most memorable moments of a round are almost always against the odds. They are almost always the result of a wayward shot. The Zen Golfer does not seek danger but welcomes the opportunity it provides. Adversity builds character. It is only from the edge that one appreciates the infinite. Only from the precipice can one envision the depths. It is only when we wander from the path that we discover the illusive keys to greater understanding. It is only when we test the limits that we illuminate our souls. There are no limits save those we impose on ourselves. There are no boundaries save those we have constructed. Break the boundaries. Accept the challenge. Welcome adversity. Embrace it.

LESSON SIXTEEN

Golf Embraces the Simple

In the beginning was the knobby and the feathery: A solid hickory stick and a skin wrapped ball of feathers. In the beginning it was no more complicated than gripping the club and striking the ball. Too often the golfer, absorbed in a thousand thoughts both technical and esoteric, forgets the most fundamental swing thought of all: Hit the ball.

We have all observed the beginning golfer after a half hour lesson on the techniques of the game. We can verbalize his mental process as he wipes his brow and addresses the ball: Left arm straight, right shoulder down, shift weight, elbow in and keep your head down. By the time the litany ends he has forgotten its beginning. We want desperately to advise: Just hit the ball. But we know he would not understand.

It is never as simple as it seems and it is never as complicated. It is said nature embraces the simple. Golf is nature; therefore golf embraces the simple.

When in doubt return to the game's most basic form: Grasp your knobby and strike your feathery. Even a master cannot hold three thoughts while striking the ball. The rest of us can barely hold two. Keep it simple and enjoy the round.

LESSON SEVENTEEN

The Garden of Earth is Heaven

Is there golf in heaven? No doubt. Heaven is the garden of earth where the game of golf is played. How do you choose to conduct yourself in paradise? Will you lose patience with your fellow players? Will you set yourself above others? Will you vent your frustrations on those around you? Will you take pleasure in the misfortunes of others? Will you rant and rave and curse the sacred sphere? Will you muddy the rules and miscount your score as if it really matters? You are in the garden. Behave accordingly. Always be aware of others. Acknowledge golfer's karma. Replace divots, repair ball marks and leave the sand trap better than you found it. Allow the hurried group behind you to play through. There is no hurry in paradise. Be patient. Give praise where praise is due. Be understanding of other's shortcomings. Be humble. Take your penalties with a contented smile. The sun will rise and fall, the great wheel of life will continue to turn and another round awaits you. Smell the flowers, breath the air and enjoy your time in the garden.

The expansive sky does not obstruct
The floating white clouds
Shitou Xiqian, 700-790

LESSON EIGHTEEN

Clear your Mind

The human mind cannot hold more than three simultaneous thoughts without impairing coordinated physical activity. With an activity as complex as the golf swing, it is best to begin with a blank slate. When the mind is clear the Zen Golfer can achieve a level of focus far beyond that of the average golfer.

While it is often impossible, it is ideal to begin a round of golf clear of the worries, pressures and problems of everyday life. Breathe deeply and focus on the trees, the wind and the natural beauty of the round. With each exhalation let go of the worries, let go the appointments, let go the tension and mental processes. Visualize the letting go. Watch your worries exit your body and rise above the tree line like rings of smoke, fading in the distance. Focus on an abstraction: See the energy lines of the fairway, the roundness of the ball, the sway of a pendulum. When the mind is free of conscious thought, let the round begin.

In the middle of a round, if you find it hard to concentrate, you should return to this basic: the blank mind. Never carry the thought of your last shot into the next. Clear your mind and begin each shot anew.

Zen be with you.

ABOUT THE AUTHOR

Jack Random has lived both an ordinary and extraordinary life. His roots firmly planted in the fertile central valley of California, he has marched the streets in protest, haunted jazz town bars, read poetry in cafes and town squares, strutted his hour upon the stage, crisscrossed the country by air, rail, highway and thumb, mourned at Wounded Knee, gazed into the eyes of the crow at Grand Canyon, and paid tribute at the grave of Geronimo. He has labored in the fields of plenty, toiled on the assembly line, pursued higher education, and attempted to enlighten children in the public schools. He has been a pilgrim and a seeker of truth. He is married to the love of his life. All the while he has chronicled his thoughts and revelations in words: plays, poetry, novels, stories and essays.

He is the author of *Wasichu: The Killing Spirit*, *Number Nine: The Adventures of Jake Jones and Ruby Daulton*, *A Patriot Dirge*, *Pawns to Players* (Crow Dog Press), *Ghost Dance Insurrection* (Dry Bones Press) and the *Jazzman Chronicles* (Crow Dog Press).

www.ingramcontent.com/pod-product-compliance
Lightning Source LLC
LaVergne TN
LVHW051728080426
835511LV00018B/2936